JUSTICE PERVERTED

William B. Crawford with Alstory Simon on the evening of October 30, 2014, Simon's first night of freedom after fifteen years in prison. Crawford is not only the author of this book but also an actor in the saga it details. For a full list of the many individuals whose stories are part of this one, see pages 214–223.

JUSTICE PERVERTED

How The
Innocence Project
at Northwestern University's
Medill School of Journalism
Sent an Innocent Man
to Prison

WILLIAM B. CRAWFORD

This narrative is dedicated to Marty Preib, a Chicago policeman, author, and blogger whose indefatigable and fearless drive went a long way in helping to unmask the injustice visited on Alstory Simon.

Justice Perverted: How The Innocence Project at Northwestern University's Medill School of Journalism Sent an Innocent Man to Prison
© Copyright 2015, William B. Crawford

First Edition   ISBN 13: 978-1-937484-36-1

AMIKA PRESS   466 Central AVE #23 Northfield IL 60093   847 920 8084
info@amikapress.com   Available for purchase on amikapress.com

Edited by John Manos. Front cover photograph from freeimages.com. Frontispiece photograph by Shawn Rech. Author photograph by William Crawford III.

Acknowledgements

Justice Perverted: How The Innocence Project at Northwestern University's Medill School of Journalism Sent an Innocent Man to Prison would not have been possible without the enduring assistance of three individuals. First and foremost my wife, Marci Abraham-Crawford, whose unyielding support allowed this four-year effort to reach a successful conclusion.

The two others: retired Alcohol, Tobacco and Firearms agents Jimmy Delorto and Johnny Mazzola without whom Alstory Simon never would have been freed from his wrongful incarceration. The two former agents, working as licensed private investigators, were the first to discover the injustice imposed on Alstory Simon, the first to identify those responsible for the injustice, and the first to bring the miscarriage to the public's attention.

Table
of Contents

Author's Note

This story follows a trail of monumental injustice. At its core is this simple fact: Through the efforts of the Innocence Project at Northwestern University's renowned Medill School of Journalism, an innocent man named Alstory Simon was framed for murders committed by a man named Anthony Porter.

The murders occurred in 1982. Porter was convicted of the crimes in 1983. Early in 1999, owing to the work of the Innocence Project and what can only be characterized as a wholesale collapse of ethical standards on the parts of prosecutors and a defense attorney alike, along with thoughtless cheerleading from the media and a series of political decisions, Porter was freed and subsequently pardoned. Later in 1999, Simon took Porter's place behind bars. Simon remained there for fifteen years.

He might be incarcerated still were it not for two private investigators named James Delorto and John Mazzola. Until around 2010, no one else paid much attention to Simon's plight. But when I was examining a different situation, I met Delorto and Mazzola.

In late summer 2009, I got a call from John Sheehan, an old friend who asked me if I would meet with Bob Dwyer, a Chicago policeman who had been wrongly accused of engaging in torture in the arrest of a man named Madison Hobley. Sheehan said that

Dwyer and his partner, James Lotito, arrested Hobley on January 6, 1987. They took him to Area Two headquarters where Hobley confessed to setting fire the night before to an apartment building in the 1100 block of East 82nd Street. The fire took the lives of Hobley's wife, his infant son, and five other residents.

In 1990 a jury convicted Hobley of seven counts of felony murder, one count of arson, and seven counts of aggravated arson. He was sentenced to death. However, the case was remanded to the lower court by the Illinois Supreme Court in 1998 for an evidentiary hearing after lawyers for Hobley argued that Hobley had confessed only after he had been handcuffed and beaten by Dwyer and other police officers at Area Two headquarters and that his captors had placed a typewriter bag over his head, nearly suffocating him.

Following protracted hearings before Cook County Criminal Court Judge Dennis Porter beginning in 2002, Porter denied Hobley's request for a new trial. Hobley's attorneys appealed again, this time to the Illinois Prisoner Review Board, which conducts hearings on such requests and makes confidential recommendations to the governor. On January 9, 2003, Governor George Ryan granted Hobley a full pardon, saying his conviction was based on "flawed evidence."

Upon his release, Hobley filed a lawsuit against the City of Chicago for his wrongful incarceration. The City settled the suit for more than $7 million, despite protestations from Dwyer and others that the City defend the case.

Bob Dwyer and I met at a coffee shop in suburban LaGrange where he confirmed Sheehan's account, though with far more specificity, asserting that Hobley had confessed voluntarily to the arson of the building in which he and his wife, his infant son, and the five other victims had lived. After I agreed to look into the Hobley case, Dwyer told me that the entire case record was in the

Batavia offices of two retired Alcohol, Firearm and Tobacco federal agents, Jimmy Delorto and Johnny Mazzola, who now worked as licensed private investigators for several lawyers and law firms.

After introducing myself to Delorto and Mazzola and asking them if I could borrow records of the Hobley case, Delorto replied, "We have all the Hobley materials. You are welcome to take what you need. But I will tell you this. You are looking at the wrong case."

I made three or four trips to their Batavia office for additional Hobley files, and each time Delorto told me, "Whatever you need is right here. But you're looking at the wrong case."

"So what case should I be looking at?" I finally asked.

"The Alstory Simon case," Delorto said.

"Who in the hell is Alstory Simon?" I replied.

"Alstory Simon is doing thirty-seven years in state prison for a double homicide that was committed by Anthony Porter."

After providing me with a broad outline of the case and the role Northwestern University's Medill School of Journalism had played in it, Delorto piqued my curiosity. But then Delorto told me that Simon was innocent even though he had pleaded guilty to the double homicide and had apologized to the mother of one of the victims as he was being sentenced. I immediately said I would be taking a pass. Innocent people don't confess to a double homicide and meekly agree to a thirty-seven-year prison term.

Then Delorto and Mazzola handed me key materials in the case, grand jury transcripts, affidavits, and, above all, the entire transcript of Alstory Simon's plea and sentencing hearing in the fall of 1999. I realized immediately that Jimmy was correct. I was looking at the wrong case.

This led directly to the Internet publication of "Chimera" in 2010. This online report is roughly 35,000 words. It is based on the underlying public record, as is this book. It was my main contribution to the effort to free Alstory Simon: I stitched together the many parts of the tangled Simon injustice into a linear yarn. "Chimera's" publication helped bring together an ad hoc team that was determined to get a hearing for Simon. That team included Delorto and Mazzola; attorneys Terry Ekl, James Sotos, and Andy Hale; Marty Preib, a Chicago policeman, author, and creator of the blog *Crooked City;* Paul Pompian, a Chicagoan who became a successful Hollywood producer before his unfortunate death in 2014; and Shawn Rech, a Cleveland producer of documentary films who took up where the late Pompian left off.

Copies of "Chimera" were sent to hundreds of individuals, including former U.S. Attorneys in Chicago, leading defense attorneys and prosecutors, virtually every investigative or crime reporter employed by Midwest, West Coast, and East Coast newspapers and periodicals, select members of the electronic media, and even certain members of the general public. Copies also were sent to every faculty member at Northwestern's Medill School of Journalism, Media, Integrated Marketing Communications (as the venerable journalism school was renamed in 2006) and to every professor at three Chicago-area law schools—Northwestern, the University of Chicago, and John Marshall.

The report received several different receptions. The general public responded with puzzlement. The legal community offered stony silence. The Northwestern faculty reacted with unalloyed hostility. So did the press, which for years had been championing the work of a former Medill professor named David Protess and his Innocence Project, with its ever-changing groups of students.

One of the most interesting responses came from Professor David Protess himself, to whom I e-mailed a copy of "Chimera" in 2010 and followed up with a request for an interview. He replied via e-mail, beginning with a list of every address I'd called home over the previous thirty years, including my current address.

"Tell me which address you are presently living at and I will send

Porter and his friends to pay you a visit," the professor wrote.[1] Not a serious threat, to be sure. Just the same, the irony is delicious. Protess and his students expended a lot of time and energy freeing Porter from "wrongful" imprisonment for a double homicide for which he was supposedly innocent. Yet when Protess wanted to imply a threat of violence, he invoked the name of Anthony Porter.

Some members of the media were invested in the conclusions that "Chimera" disputed, and perhaps predictably, many chose to go on the attack. For example, *Tribune* columnist Eric Zorn referred to me as a "dyspeptic former investigative reporter." But aggressive reactions to any criticism of Protess or the Innocence Project were not new, at least for Zorn. Years earlier he had disparaged Simon's attorneys, Ekl and Sotos. His January 5, 2006, column ran under the headline, "Two Lawyers Cast in Unlikely Roles as Crusaders." Zorn noted, "Sotos is the attorney for Jon Burge, the former Chicago police commander who was fired for torturing a murder suspect" and was later sentenced to prison for perjury. He described Ekl as "a former prosecutor with close ties to the DuPage County Republican" establishment—as if that fact is sufficient to make a reasonable person question Ekl's integrity and desire for justice.

The disinclination of the press to take a closer look at Protess's work cannot be blamed solely on hostility to "Chimera" and the small group of people who felt a right had been wronged when Simon replaced Porter in prison. Several members of the local press had become virtual cheerleaders for the Innocence Project, calling Protess regularly to find out what new developments may have taken place in the investigation du jour.

A June 11, 1996, Zorn column underscores this point.

"Frequently over the past several months I'd call Northwestern University journalism professor David Protess and ask: 'So what have the kids come up with?' It was usually something and it was usually big—a recantation, a confession, an affidavit, a key document. Protess would give me and reporters from Channel Five the leads, which were easy to re-report, and we would then publicly advance the story of the apparent miscarriage of justice" of the latest Innocence Project endeavor.

The fact that a given columnist supported the ideals and goals of the Innocence Project is not the issue. The problem is that every bit of information in "Chimera" and in this book is and was in the public record. The news media's support of Porter's "exoneration" might not have been quite so universal if reporters had read the grand jury and trial testimony against him. Had members of the media been a little more diligent, they might have asked questions about Simon's conviction, because they would have known that no witness put him at the scene of the murder— whereas multiple witnesses put Porter there and identified him as the killer. Some members of the media might have concluded that Simon was going to prison based on a false confession—had they bothered to examine the circumstances of his confession.

Similar questions about diligence come to mind regarding the state's attorney's office. I sat down with just one former assistant state's attorney following the distribution of "Chimera." In fall 2010, I met with Bob Milan, an attorney who worked under then-State's Attorney Dick Devine and had become one of his trusted aides. When Devine opted not to run for reelection, Milan tossed his hat into the 2008 race with Devine's endorsement, but he lost to Anita Alvarez in the primary after picking up only five percent of the vote.

Nothing came of my meeting with Milan. But there is an interesting sidebar to the Milan anecdote that occurred long before he and I met.

After Simon confessed and was sentenced, Milan, with the blessing of his boss, announced a sweeping set of reforms within

Devine's office. The centerpiece of Milan's reforms, of all things, was creation of an educational program for prosecutors in the nearly-900-person Cook County State's Attorney's office to teach those prosecutors how to detect false confessions and prevent wrongful convictions. By 2003, Milan had become such an expert in this field that he ultimately flew all around the country to lecture public prosecutors on how to spot phony confessions.

"Innocent people do confess to horrible crimes they didn't commit," Milan told a group of colleagues gathered for one of the newly launched training sessions in early 2003.

The session included a review of red flags prosecutors should look for when a suspect is confessing. Chief among those red flags: the defendant's age and mental and psychological condition. This would seem to be the very concern in Simon's case, as is described in chapter 5. Milan also warned that state's attorneys should not develop tunnel vision after a "confession," but should ensure that the story a suspect offers matches clues in the case.

Had this advice been applied to Alstory Simon, he might never have gone to prison.

By late 2010 the ad hoc group began to coalesce around a resurgent effort to expose Medill's wrongdoing and to free Alstory Simon by proving his innocence. Gradually momentum built up. Meaningfully, individuals who had been in the pool that night in 1982 and had witnessed Porter shoot his two victims began to come forward as word circulated that a genuine, renewed attempt to win freedom for Simon was at last gaining headway.

All I can now say is I am proud to have been a part of it. As Delorto told me nearly five years ago, I was looking at the wrong case. Thankfully, he and Mazzola never stopped looking at it.

----

1   See the *Crooked City* blog (martin-preib-b7is.squarespace.com/news) for a discussion of this eccentric e-mail.

Introduction

More than thirty years ago, a double homicide occurred in Chicago in late summer, after the Bud Billiken Day Parade, in the pool area of a public park on the city's South Side. The victims lived in the Chicago Housing Authority's Robert Taylor Homes. The assailant lived in an apartment a block or two from the Taylor public projects. It could be said that the assailant and his victims were all residents of hell.

Built in 1962, the Taylor Homes stretched from 39th to 54th Streets, facing east over Lake Michigan. At the time it was built, the complex was the largest public housing project in the United States. Before the project was razed at the turn of the last century (the last of its twenty-eight buildings demolished only in 2007), more than 27,000 impoverished men, women, and children of African-American descent, living in 4,300 apartments, called those projects home.

Daily life in "The Jets," as many residents referred to the Taylor homes, was unyielding, hard as granite, chaotic. It was almost unimaginably violent. The vast majority of residents struggled from one day to the next, eking out existences on public-aid checks while dodging bullets, thugs, and con artists. Police and fire department personnel in those days were routinely accused of failing to respond to emergency calls there. The accusations were often valid; first responders sometimes ignored calls from the area—out of fear they were being set up for robbery or ambush.

For these reasons, the double homicide pretty much was ignored by the city's ink and electronic press. After all, as the industry adage asserts, news is a man biting a dog, not the reverse. Thus, it was tough to imagine way back then that the killer—a violent, semiliterate, high-school dropout raised with ten siblings by a single mother—would morph into a poster child for all that was thought to be in error about the death penalty in Illinois and across the country.

It also was a challenge to imagine way back then that the offender and his double homicide would, in the fullness of time, come to impugn the reputation of Northwestern University's renowned Medill School of Journalism, a former professor there, several of his former students, and a faculty member of the university's Law School—that the double homicide and the offender would become a blot on the university's 1851 escutcheon: *Quaecumque Sunt Vera,* "Whatsoever Things Are True."

And no one could have possibly forecast at the time that the future road traveled by the assailant—a man named Anthony Porter—would intersect with another individual by the name of Alstory Simon in a tragic, twisted way. Indeed, in a Dickensian kind of way, with Porter ultimately freed from death row for the double homicide for which he had been convicted and Alstory Simon sentenced to thirty-seven years in Danville State Prison for the double homicide Simon did not commit.

As this improbable story unfolded, chapter after chapter, one level after another, it would cast long shadows across Illinois personalities who would get caught up in it one way or another, directly or indirectly. A Cook County state's attorney, top assistants in that office, an Illinois governor, current and former Illinois state judges, a Chicago-based private investigator, defense attorneys, and even a Chicago mayor. All would get dinged in this protracted tale of monstrous injustice.

Supporting actors in this tragicomedy? Certain members of the print and electronic media, especially in Chicago, who routinely regurgitated information handed off to them by a Northwestern journalism professor without any effort on the part of these reporters to check whether the underlying facts supported the professor's claims.

Thomas Epach was the chief of the Criminal Division in the Cook County State's Attorney's office years ago when this story was heading into what everyone believed was its final chapter. His view of the sorry mess?

"It was Cook County's worst day," Epach declared. "Nothing like this had ever happened before, certainly not in Cook County. Here an assistant Cook County prosecutor spends weeks before a grand jury calling witnesses and in the end proving once again that Porter, not Simon, committed the murders. Then a few weeks later that same prosecutor stands before the sentencing judge and doesn't utter a word about that evidence exculpating Simon as Simon is being sentenced to prison for Porter's crime."

Epach, now retired, added, "I'll tell you this. A journalism professor leading a bunch of naïve students around by their noses? A travesty. The Good Lord has saved a special place in hell for all those responsible for this wrongdoing. That special place is right next to the furnace."

1

Arrest and Murder Conviction of Anthony Porter

In mid-August, more than three decades ago, an assailant pulled out a revolver and fatally shot Marilyn Green and her fiancé, Jerry Hillard, as the couple sat high up in the spectators' bleachers overlooking the Olympic-sized swimming pool in Washington Park on Chicago's South Side.

Grasping her neck in a vain effort to staunch profuse bleeding, Green staggered down the bleachers and exited the pool area before crumpling onto the park pavement about a block away. Green was rushed to Provident Hospital stretched out on the rear seat of a Chicago Police Department squad car where she was pronounced dead on arrival.

Hillard was found lying unconscious on his back in the bleachers where the couple had been sitting. Still breathing, Hillard was transported to the hospital by Chicago Fire Department ambulance. He died on the operating table at the University of Chicago's Billings Hospital soon after emergency medical technicians had wheeled him on a stretcher through the emergency room doors.

It was August 15, 1982. The shooting occurred at about one in the morning beneath a clear, star-studded sky; the night was warm, seventy-five degrees and humid.

An autopsy by the Cook County Medical Examiner's Office concluded that Hillard, eighteen, of 5323 S. Federal Street, had been shot twice in the head. Green, nineteen, of 37 W. Garfield Boulevard, the mother of two toddlers, had been struck three times— twice in the neck and once in the hand. The autopsy reports, signed by Dr. Joanne Richmond, concluded that both victims had been shot at point-blank range.

The weapon, identified by police ballistics experts as a .38-caliber revolver, never was recovered. Chicago Police Department Mobile Crime Lab personnel, called to the scene shortly after the incident, reported that "a small, pin-type jewelry piece with a small, silver-colored chain with silver-colored lock," had been recovered from beneath Hillard's body. From that, police initially concluded that armed robbery was the motive behind the shootings.

The double homicide occurred a few hours following the conclusion of a far happier event: the August 14 Bud Billiken Day Parade and Picnic, a largely African-American annual affair launched in 1929 by Robert Sengstacke Abbott, publisher of the *Chicago Defender*, the city's only black newspaper. Named after "the Billiken," the guardian angel of little children according to Chinese legend, the parade consisted of high-school marching bands, floats, tumblers, dancers, drill teams, an occasional cartoon character, and, of course, well-known personalities and politicians of broad stripes, ranging over the years from Muhammad Ali and Bozo the Clown to Presidents Harry S. Truman and Barack Obama.

The Bud Billiken Day Parade, a much-anticipated outing, takes place on the second Saturday of August each year. Hundreds of thousands of adults and children line the street as the parade courses along its traditional route. Starting at 35th Street, the parade proceeds south on Dr. Martin Luther King Jr. Drive and ends at 51st Street, in Washington Park where, by tradition, throngs of friends and family cap the day off with cookouts and partying well into the night.

At the time of the 1 A.M. shootings, Washington Park had all but emptied out, with well-filled picnickers and partyers having returned to their homes for the night. All but several dozen men, women, and youngsters, that is, who had opted instead to sneak into the park pool—which by Chicago Park District rules was locked at sundown—either to socialize and kick back, like Hillard and Green, or to cool off with a dip in the pool. Police were well aware of regular nighttime entries to the locked pool area, but they customarily looked the other way so long as there were no reports of trouble.

Within several hours of the shootings, Chicago police Area One Violent Crime detectives Charles Salvatore and Dennis Gray had located three individuals who had been in the pool area that morning and who all fingered a young man named Anthony Porter. They were William Taylor, thirty-nine, of 210 E. 55th Street; Taylor's friend Henry Williams, twenty-nine, who lived in a basement apartment with his mother, at 5428 S. Prairie Avenue; and Kenneth Edwards, twenty-two, of 328 E. 56th Street.

On August 16, a day after the shootings, Edwards, who had been taken to Area One headquarters, identified Porter in Chicago Police Photo Album #813, mug shot 29-C, as the offender. So did Williams. Two days later, at a five-person lineup supervised by Area One Sergeant John Fitzgerald, Taylor identified participant #1—Anthony Porter—as the person "he saw shoot Marilyn Green and Jerry Hillard."

A variety of people who were in the Washington Park pool that night said another man had been with Porter and had left the bleachers with him after he shot the couple. This individual has never been identified, but none of the witnesses claimed the unidentified accomplice did the shooting.

In addition, there was Anthony Liace, a six-year veteran of the Chicago Police Department who, responding to a police communications call of a shooting in Washington Park, arrived in time to stop Porter as he was fleeing from the pool and frisk him. And though the pat down turned up nothing, Liace just over a year later would provide a crucial evidentiary link, telling a criminal court jury about his encounter with Porter only minutes after Liace had responded to the 911 call and arrived outside the pool.

But the witness list did not end there. Police also had interviewed three other young men who had been in the pool, had seen Porter there, and had given incriminating statements against Porter and his involvement in the homicides. The three were identified as Michael Woodfork, Eugene Beckwith, and Mark Senior.

And there was more. Police arriving for the day shift on the morning of August 15 were greeted by the Chicago Police Department's daily bulletin, in which a black-and-white, full-face photograph of Anthony Porter was prominently featured in the center of the front page. Beneath Porter's photo was a short paragraph alerting police that Porter was wanted on an aggravated battery warrant, #CD19340, stemming from the unprovoked shooting of a man in the head, and that the suspect was considered armed and dangerous. That shooting—in which the victim survived with a graze across the forehead—had occurred just two weeks before, on August 1, only three blocks from the Washington Park pool, and in broad daylight.

"Anthony Porter, aka Michael Goodman, aka Anthony Goodman, 5608 S. Michigan Avenue, male black, twenty-seven, five feet six inches tall, 170 pounds, medium build, medium complexion, black hair, mustache, processed hair, wanted for aggravated battery, a known gang member. Frequents areas of 5326 S. State Street, corner of 56th and Michigan Avenue. Considered armed and dangerous," the bulletin asserted.

A day after the shooting, Detectives Salvatore and Gray, acting on a tip that the offender was hiding in his home, visited Porter's apartment at 5608 S. Michigan Avenue. Though police did not find Porter there, they did find Tyrone Horton, twenty-two, aka "Loco," an unemployed laborer and a friend of Porter's. Horton was asleep in a bedroom.

After bringing Horton to Area One for further questioning, the detectives developed evidence that Horton and a woman by the name of "Zena" had funneled cash from a Gladys Rutledge, 5201 S. Federal Street, to Porter early on August 16 to help him support himself while hiding from police. Police charged Horton with aiding a fugitive.

Following Horton's arrest and after reviewing the evidence, talking to Taylor and Williams and other pool witnesses, and visiting the murder scene, Assistant Cook County State's Attorney David Kerstein, assigned to the Night Felony Review Section, approved an arrest warrant for Porter, charging him with the murders of Hillard and Green. After the August 16 warrant had also been approved by Kerstein's supervisor, prosecutor Thomas Roche, the warrant was signed by Cook County Circuit Judge Anthony Costa, and an all-points bulletin went out for Porter's arrest.

The next day Porter turned himself in at police headquarters, then located at 1121 S. State Street. His uncle Robert; aunts Thelma and Helen; his mother, Clara Mae; and father, Willie, accompanied him because, Porter said, much later, he was fearful of the police. As he was being read his Miranda rights, Porter told authorities they had the wrong man. No way he was involved, the suspect said, because around 10 P.M., on August 14, he and three friends—Kenneth Doyle, aka, "Fat Luke," another young man called "Tobar," and Tyrone Horton were chilling out at "The Hole," a cavernous outdoor area situated among the Robert Taylor Homes, 2300 S. State Street.

About a half-hour later Porter said he and Fat Luke departed from the others, walked to the nearby Midway Liquors, bought a bottle of Richard's wine, and returned to Porter's apartment where they polished off the wine. They did not leave his apartment until the following morning, with Fat Luke sleeping over, Porter said.

Porter was arraigned September 9, 1982, before Criminal Court Judge Robert Skoldowski on an indictment charging him with the murders of Jerry Hillard and Marilyn Green, armed robbery, unlawful restraint, and unlawful use of a weapon. In the ensuing weeks, the evidence against the defendant continued to mount, with authorities eventually locating more than a half-dozen witnesses to the shooting. Evidence was becoming so overwhelming that many observers believed Porter and his attorney would strike a plea bargain instead of going to trial and risking a guilty verdict and a sentence of death.

After Porter's surrender, authorities learned that he had a lengthy rap sheet and had done time in state prison for armed robbery and other felonies. More importantly, he was wanted on the arrest warrant charging him with the unrelated shooting that had occurred two weeks before the double homicide at the Washington Park pool. In the earlier incident, according to the arrest warrant, Porter shot Earl Lewis, thirty-one, in the head in broad daylight on August 1, as the victim sat with his dog on the front stoop of a building three blocks from Washington Park.

(Porter pleaded guilty to an aggravated battery charge stemming from that shooting almost exactly a year later, on August 8, 1983, a couple of weeks before his murder trial began. Cook County Circuit Court Judge Donald Lowery sentenced him to six years for that crime.)

The evidence accumulating, the State's case against Porter moved forward to trial at the end of August 1983 when a jury had been chosen and sworn in by Judge Skoldowski. During opening statements, Assistant State's Attorney Paul Szigetvari painted a gruesome picture for jurors of how Porter gunned down Hillard and Green, a "pair of lovers" soon to be married, whose great misfortune it was to seek relief from the summer heat by scaling the north end of the pool bleachers and seating themselves on the top row.

Referencing trial evidence to come, Szigetvari said Henry Williams, a key State witness, would testify that Porter entered the pool with a drawn .38-caliber pistol, approached Williams, "put that gun square to his forehead," reached in and removed two dollars from Williams's pocket, and then mounted the bleachers where he gunned down Hillard and Green in an apparent robbery. "When he got to Hillard the gun was upraised and Porter discharged the gun shooting Hillard. With this, Jerry Hillard fell back. Porter stood over him and fired one more shot into his body."

As for Green, Szigetvari went on, "Porter shot her twice in the neck. Marilyn struggled up and went out of the bleachers section," and, holding her neck, "gurgling blood," she staggered out of the pool complex and into Washington Park.

When it was the defense's turn, Akim Gursel, who represented Porter, acknowledged that his client was a street gang member and a convicted felon but asserted that those facts were irrelevant and that Porter was innocent of the Washington Park slayings. Instead of addressing the State's evidence head-on, Gursel appealed to his listeners' better natures, reminding them of their sacred duties as citizens and jurors and urging them to abide by their consciences, to eschew outside influences, and to return a verdict based solely on the facts.

The State's most important witnesses were William Taylor, who worked for a temporary employment agency, and his friend Henry Williams, a part-time college student. One after the other, they provided testimony that must have left jurors scratching their heads and asking themselves why they had been summoned to

Judge Skoldowski's courtroom in the first place.

Taylor, the first to be called by the prosecution, set the stage for jurors, telling them that he and Williams scaled the fence surrounding the closed Washington Park pool, stripped down to the trunks worn beneath their clothes, and went for a swim around one o'clock that warm and humid morning. They swam in the Olympic pool, the largest of the three park pools. He said he lost track of his buddy, climbed out of the pool and was drying himself off when he heard the sound of a gunshot.

"I looked up at the bleachers to see if Henry was there and I saw a man being shot," Taylor testified, under questioning by Szigetvari.

Taylor said Porter was standing two feet away from his victim, his left arm extended, holding a gun in his left hand. He testified that he saw the victim fall back onto the bleachers. With his left arm still extended, still holding the gun, Porter pointed the weapon down at his victim and fired another round into his body, the witness said.

Moments after the shootings, Taylor said Porter descended the bleachers and made his way to the exit, running so close to Taylor that Taylor was able to get a good look at Porter's face. He recognized Porter as the man Taylor frequently spotted in the neighborhood but gave a wide berth to because of his reputation for unbridled violence. Taylor testified that he could see that Porter was carrying a revolver. Police arrived soon after, and Taylor said at their request he helped carry Hillard to a Chicago Fire Department ambulance.

Williams, a nursing student at Malcolm X College in Chicago, took the stand next and delivered equally compelling testimony. He told jurors that as he pulled himself out of the pool, Porter, whom he also had come to know from the neighborhood, appeared out of nowhere with a drawn pistol, robbed him of two dollars, and then mounted the bleachers. He told jurors he saw Porter and the victims standing four feet apart at the top of the bleachers and that he, Williams, jumped the fence just as he heard the sound of gunshots.

In cross-examination Gursel sought to diminish the credibility of the State's leadoff witnesses, first suggesting that the lighting at the pool was too poor for a proper identification. When Taylor answered that the pool area was lit up "like a professional football game," by two thirty-foot towers equipped with ten banks of lights on each tower, Gursel changed tack.

Acknowledging that his client was a member of a street gang, Gursel suggested that Taylor's adverse testimony had its genesis in the fact that Taylor was a member of a rival neighborhood gang called the Disciples. Gursel's course correction proved no more fruitful.

GURSEL: Sir, aren't you a Disciple?

TAYLOR: No, I am not.

GURSEL: Haven't you been a Disciple?

TAYLOR: No, I have not.

GURSEL: Are any of your friends Disciples?

TAYLOR: No, they are not.

Before he was finished with the witness, Gursel elicited the admission from Taylor that he had not been immediately forthcoming with police during initial questioning about what he had seen the night of the shootings. Taylor explained that he knew Porter to be a man given to eruptions of unprovoked violence, saying that he saw Porter mug two elderly people in front of Taylor's house. Taylor said his initial reluctance to cooperate with police stemmed from the fact he lived with his ninety-five-year-old great-grandmother, and he feared that if he became a known snitch in the shooting deaths, Porter's brothers would come looking for him or, worse yet, inflict harm on his great-grandmother.

And, of course, there was the chain-of-evidence testimony offered by Anthony Liace, one of the first Chicago Police officers to have arrived at the Washington Park pool only minutes after central communications sent out a call of a shooting there. After identifying Porter in the courtroom, Liace testified that Porter, fleeing from the pool, ran into Liace's arms. After patting down Porter and finding nothing on his person, Liace said he let Porter go and raced to the pool.

The State rested after three days of testimony. Now it was Gursel's turn. The defense called only four witnesses, the most bizarre and candid of whom proved to be Kenneth Doyle, 20, of 5323 S. Michigan Avenue. Doyle, Porter's main alibi witness, said he was known generally on the street as "Fat Luke" and acknowledged that he, Porter, and Jerry Hillard, one of the victims, were members of the same gang and were good friends.

Single and unemployed, Fat Luke testified that on the eve of the murders, he visited the defendant in his mother's apartment at 5606 S. Michigan Aveue, around 10 P.M. When he arrived, he testified, several people were already present, including Porter, Porter's mother, and his brother Michael. Porter's sister-in-law Georgia, whose last name the witness did not know, and Tobar, whose birth name the witness also did not know, were present as well, along with two or three children. Cards and children's games were being played, Doyle testified.

Porter, Doyle, Tobar, and one or two others soon repaired to the apartment's rear porch where Doyle said he consumed large amounts of Wild Irish Rose. At 2 A.M. sharp, Doyle said they walked to the nearby Taylor Homes playground, where they "sat around and got high," drinking more alcohol and smoking reefers until 9 A.M. when the group broke up.

"Just sitting out there and talking, talking to each other about the old days, old times. That is it," Doyle replied when asked by

Gursel what the primary subject of the evening's conversation was.

Under cross-examination by Cook County co-prosecutor Paula Daleo, Doyle was asked questions for which he clearly was not prepared, and he offered up responses that surely must have confused or even dumbfounded the jurors.

After confirming that he was a member of the Cobra Stones, which Doyle said controlled turf between State Street and Indiana Avenue around 2300 South, Daleo asked the witness what his position was in the gang's hierarchy.

DOYLE: Well, I'm not really no chief or nothing like that. But you know I just go along with the rest of the fellows.

DALEO: What do the rest of the fellows do, Mr. Doyle?

DOYLE: They gangbang.

DALEO: Tell the ladies and gentlemen of the jury what it means to gangbang.

DOYLE: Fighting.

DALEO: Fighting, what else do they do?

DOYLE: Whatever is necessary.

DALEO: What does that mean, Mr. Doyle, whatever is necessary?

DOYLE: Whatever it comes down to. That is all I can say.

DALEO: Well, we know that means fighting, right?

DOYLE: Yes, ma'am.

DALEO: Does that mean killing?

DOYLE: If it's necessary.

DALEO: It's part of your belief and part of your rules of the gang to come in here and testify for one of your brothers who is on trial, right?

DOYLE: Yes, ma'am.

Equally devastating for the defense was when under cross-examination by Daleo, the witness admitted that two days after the 1982 shootings, he told Chicago Police Department homicide detectives Charles Salvatore and Dennis Gray, who were heading the investigation, that he had been drinking with the defendant, but only until about 10:30 P.M., at which time he went home and went to sleep, a 180-degree turnabout from his trial testimony.

DALEO: Do you also remember telling them [Salvatore and Gray] at that time, 10:30 in the evening, that you went back to your apartment and spent the remainder of the night, that is, August 14, 1982, with your mother?

DOYLE: Yes ma'am, I sure did tell them that.

Moreover, though it was never brought out at trial, because Porter declined to take the stand, it will be remembered that minutes after Porter surrendered to police on August 17, 1982, he told police that he and Fat Luke had purchased a bottle of Richard's wine at Midway Liquors earlier in the evening and returned to Porter's apartment where they consumed the wine and went to sleep, with Fat Luke sleeping over.

Gursel called two more witnesses. Eric Werner, a professional photographer, testified about lighting conditions at the park and introduced pictures he had taken of the pool area more than one year after the shootings—a week before the trial. As a final witness, Gursel called Georgia Moody, the common-law wife of one of Porter's brothers.

In a second damaging, though less so, setback for the defense, Moody—in direct contradiction to Doyle—testified that to her knowledge, Porter and Doyle did not go out on the porch and were not drinking. She testified that Porter and Doyle remained in Porter's mother's house all day and well into the evening, playing "children's cards games like pitty pat," with Moody's eight-year-old son, Octavia, and her twelve-year old daughter, Kanetka. She said Porter and Doyle exited the apartment around 2:30 A.M.

Gursel rested without calling to the stand that individual in the courtroom jurors surely wanted to hear from the most: Anthony Porter, the defendant.

Final arguments commenced on September 1, the third day of trial, with Szigetvari likening Porter to a wild animal of the African savanna, circling the Washington Park pool as though it was a watering hole, looking for victims who had gathered there on a hot night to cool off. Calling the defendant a "predator," the prosecutor said Porter went to Washington Park that night because he had a "captive audience about the watering hole that, under the cover of darkness, he could rob to his heart's content."

Szigetvari concluded, telling jurors that his analogy was imperfect: "Wild predators don't kill aimlessly. They kill to survive and eat their prey."

When it was Gursel's turn, he again drifted from directly confronting evidence that had been presented by the State. In conclusion, he said his client had "engaged in criminal anti-social behavior. He's a gang member. Our city is filled with them. But that doesn't make him a murderer. That doesn't make him a murderer. That doesn't do it." Despite the beating Doyle had taken on cross-examination, Gursel reprised his testimony, reminding jurors that his client was not even in the park that night.

After all the evidence had been presented, Judge Skoldowski read a set of instructions to jurors and sent them out of the courtroom at 12:30 P.M. to begin their deliberations. A few minutes before nine o'clock that evening, the foreman sent a note that the panel had reached a verdict.

The jurors filed in and took their seats. The verdict: guilty on all counts.

In closing this segment, a point is worthy of emphasis. A year had passed since the park shootings, police had conducted their investigation, police reports had been generated, the defense had prepared its case, pretrial motions had been filed and ruled on by Skoldowski, a three-day trial had been held, and out of that flurry of activity nowhere—*nowhere*—did there emerge a witness, a police report, an allegation by the defense, or a shred of a document anywhere that suggested that a man by the name of Alstory Simon had anything to do with the crime or, indeed, that he had been anywhere near the pool that evening.

It is also worth noting, and again with regard to all those documents, there was not a single suggestion by any person or in the content of any official reports, that police had engaged in improprieties of any kind in solving this rather open-and-shut case.

There remained a final chapter in what was believed to be Porter's last journey through the Cook County legal system: a hearing to determine whether the defendant was deserving of the death penalty, which the State was seeking, and, if so, whether he was mentally fit for such punishment. The decision was to be made by the judge because Gursel had waived jury participation in the post-trial sentencing hearing.

In arguing that Porter was a candidate for the ultimate penalty, Szigetvari and Daleo called two witnesses to support their view that the Washington Park murders were not an aberration or the product of a one-time fit of rage, but that the episode was part of a broad pattern of criminal behavior and had its origins in an evil abiding deep in the defendant's soul. To that end, they called two men who had endured violent encounters with Porter.

Douglas McGhee, twenty-nine, took the stand and again returned Judge Skoldowski to the Washington Park pool. McGhee testified that on July 27, 1979, at 6:30 P.M., he was in the spectators' bleachers, doing some "bikini watching," when he mentioned to Porter, who was seated next to him but whom he did not know, that he hoped to move out of Chicago, sooner rather than later, by car or by bus. Porter replied that he had a car for sale, it was in good shape, and it was all McGhee's if he could come up with $500.

McGhee said he went home and returned a short time later

with $800 in cash. After flashing the money, he said Porter, in the presence of three or four other men and boys, knocked him to the ground and kicked him in the face and ribs repeatedly, leaving him senseless and bloodied, his face swollen and with long-term damage to one eye. As McGhee lay on the concrete, barely conscious, he said Porter reached into his pocket, grabbed the $800, and disappeared with the others. Hearing testimony revealed that at the time of the McGhee beating Porter was serving a two-year sentence of probation for bail jumping on an early 1970s robbery charge.

On October 6, 1980, the defendant pleaded guilty to the robbery of McGhee and bail jumping and was sentenced to three years in the Illinois Department of Corrections. The defendant was released from prison on November 13, 1981, and was placed on parole for two years.

Earl Lewis, the man with the dog, also testified at the penalty phase of the trial about his 1982 encounter with Porter—while Porter was on parole for the McGhee beating and robbery. Two weeks before the Washington Park homicides, three blocks away from the scene of that 1982 crime, Lewis testified that he and his sister and his sister's boyfriend were returning from the park where they had gone for a walk with Lewis's dog. Lewis said he sat down on a front stoop at 56th Street and Michigan Avenue, when Porter, whom he recognized from the neighborhood but did not know, walked past and, without provocation, kicked Lewis's dog.

Lewis said the two men exchanged words, and then Porter disappeared into a nearby building. He re-emerged minutes later with a drawn gun. He approached Lewis from behind and without saying a word, placed the gun to Lewis's head and fired one round, grazing the victim across the forehead and sending him reeling and dazed against a parked car. Lewis required medical care.

Prosecutors also introduced Porter's rap sheet into the public record during the post-trial hearing. It contained more than two dozen entries beginning in February 1972 and coming to a halt only when Porter was ordered held without bail in connection to the 1982 pool shootings. Entries included virtually every violent crime imaginable, from rape, robbery, hostage-taking, and disorderly conduct to aggravated battery, armed robbery, intimidation, and unlawful use of a weapon. During one eight-month period in the early 1980s, police questioned him three times as a suspect in three different homicides.

In mitigation, Gursel elicited testimony from Porter's mother and others seeking to spare Porter's life. They told how the defendant attended church and helped clean it, that he assisted an elderly man who was recuperating from a heart attack by taking out his garbage, and helped his grandmother, who had epileptic seizures, by cleaning her house, making her food, and seeing to it that she took her medicine.

And the defendant had challenging personal responsibilities, the judge was told. He was the father of five children—by two women with whom he had had successive relationships—who would need his guidance when he got out of prison. Clara Mae Porter also told the court of the challenges and difficulties she had faced as a single mother raising eleven children, including Porter, in the gang-infested neighborhood adjacent to the Robert Taylor Public Housing Project.

Finally, several witnesses expressed the opinion that the defendant could be "turned into a useful citizen" if he were given a chance.

At the close of the hearing, Judge Skoldowski sentenced Porter to death. Before he did so, Skoldowski, like prosecutor Szigetvari before him, likened Porter to an animal. This time, "to a shark in a frenzy of robbery, destruction, and death. You took two lives without reason," the judge said, "only to satisfy your appetite for violence."

Following the sentencing, Gursel withdrew from representing Porter, declining to file any post-trial motions let alone appeals on his client's behalf. He said he was pulling out of the case because Porter family members, who initially had agreed on a $10,000 fee, had in fact paid him only $3,000 and refused Gursel's repeated requests to pay the balance.

The Illinois Supreme Court affirmed Porter's conviction and sentence on direct appeal on February 21, 1986. From the day he was convicted in the fall of 1983, Porter spent the next seventeen years languishing in obscurity on death row in the Illinois State prison system, three-quarters of that time spent in solitary confinement for dozens upon dozens of infractions of prison rules—infractions that included attacking guards, fighting with fellow inmates, defecating in his food tray, and stopping up his cell toilet and causing its contents to overflow onto the floor of his cell and the cells of fellow death-row inmates. And on and on.

Porter awoke each morning in this solitary, bleak, and frequently violent incarceration, not knowing whether his last meal had finally arrived before being handed over to the executioner. But then slowly at first, more rapidly with time, he surfaced to become quite literally a nationwide cause célèbre for all those who believed imposition of the death penalty was in error—because jurors and jury trials were not infallible, because the taking of an eye-for-an-eye was morally indefensible, and because such action violated the U.S. Constitution's prohibition of cruel and unusual punishment.

Porter's emergence from obscurity in 1998 and 1999, came in a big way courtesy of David Protess, a professor at Northwestern University's Medill School of Journalism, one of the leading journalism schools in the country. Protess was also director of the

Medill Innocence Project, an initiative he founded in 1999, with a mandate to teach journalism students the art of reviewing and parsing death-penalty cases like Porter's to determine whether those cases had been properly investigated by police, fairly adjudicated by presiding judges, properly tried by prosecutors, and adequately defended by defense attorneys—in short, to find out whether or not authorities in the end had gotten their man.

2

Medill and the
Ford Heights Four Case

The genesis of how the paths of Anthony Porter and David Protess ultimately intersected and exploded into public view can be traced in part to the fall of 1998, and a course offered for the first time by Northwestern University's Medill School of Journalism. Titled the News Media and Capital Punishment, the course was designed and would be taught by David Protess, since 1981 an admired Medill journalism professor and, according to fellow faculty, a very capable individual possessed of supreme self-confidence, an oversized ego, and a drive to accomplish whatever goals he set for himself.

The son of Sidney and Beverly Gordon Protess and a native of Long Island, by way of Brooklyn where he was born on April 7, 1946, Protess arrived in Chicago in the mid-1960s. Early on he proved to be a prodigious academic with a deep well of energy in pursuit of certain social justice goals. He also was skilled at self-promotion, in the opinion of several Northwestern colleagues who assisted the Innocence Project (among other descriptions, colleagues have also called him hot-tempered and a master at exploiting the media). He received a B.A. in political science from Roosevelt University in 1968, an M.A. from the University of Chicago in the program of Community Organization in 1970, and a

Ph.D. in public policy from the University of Chicago four years later.

He joined the faculty of Loyola University Chicago in 1974 and served as an assistant professor of political science to 1976. He spent the next five years as research director of Chicago's Better Government Association, a privately funded watchdog group that was charged with ferreting out waste in state and local government. In 1981 he accepted an appointment as professor in Northwestern University's Medill School of Journalism.

In his personal biography, he asserts that from his youth he held a passionate interest in matters of social justice. Personally impacting on his psyche as a youngster were lingering memories of accounts of the executions of Julius and Ethel Rosenberg, who had been convicted as Soviet spies, well after that couple had been put to death in 1953. Against that backdrop, it was only natural that he settled on teaching Medill courses relating to the news media and capital punishment, legal affairs, and the law and ethics of journalism.

In addition to his teaching, he held various academic posts, including a faculty fellow at Northwestern's Institute for Policy Research and a faculty affiliate for the Joint Center for Policy Research, a dual effort between Northwestern and the University of Chicago. Despite his crowded in-class and out-of-class academic schedule, Protess still managed to find time to write and edit articles for the *Chicago Lawyer,* a monthly advocacy publication, from 1986 to 1990. Founded by Rob Warden in the late 1970s before he sold it a decade later to the Law Bulletin Publishing Company, the *Chicago Lawyer* was a tabloid that has claimed credit for exposing a half-dozen wrongful convictions, including turning early attention to four men known as the Ford Heights Four, who had been charged with a heinous crime but were later exonerated in 1996.

The newly launched course, the News Media and Capital Punishment, had two central components. The first element required the seventeen students who had enrolled in the course to study, prepare for, attend, and write about the first annual National Conference on Wrongful Convictions and the Death Penalty launched that fall. It was the first gathering of its kind since the U.S. Supreme Court had reinstated the death penalty in 1976. With the University's support, the three-day conference, beginning November 13, was to be held on Northwestern University's law-school campus on Chicago Avenue, just east of Chicago's fabled, upscale shopping area on North Michigan Avenue.

To address the second key component, the seventeen students enrolled in the course were divided into four teams, with each team reviewing the conviction of one of four different death-penalty defendants who were incarcerated in the Illinois state prison system. Each team was to determine whether a possible miscarriage of justice had occurred in the original investigation and prosecution of that inmate and write a preliminary report about the case. To the extent possible, that meant the students would be reviewing court documents; locating and interviewing critical witnesses; talking to defense attorneys, prosecutors, and detectives who had knowledge of the arrests and trials; visiting the scenes of the crimes if feasible; and basically dissecting each aspect of the conviction.

The course, approved the previous spring by Medill Dean Ken Bode, was engendered by a series of extraordinary events involving an internationally acclaimed story that was also generating conversation about a million-dollar movie contract with Disney, courtesy of efforts by Protess and Rob Warden. In 1996, Protess, Warden, three Protess students, a private investigator, and a handful of outside attorneys played varying roles in freeing from prison four wrongfully incarcerated men known as the

Ford Heights Four, who had been charged with and convicted of a horrific 1978 gang rape and double homicide.

The Ford Heights Four story of injustice is protracted, takes many twists, and contains several subplots all of which will be examined more closely in a subsequent chapter. However, for now, here are the key highlights of the case.

Dennis Williams, William Rainge, Kenneth Adams, and Verneal Jimerson were convicted of the abduction of Carol Schmal, twenty-three, and her fiancé, Lawrence Lionberg, twenty-six, from a Clark gas station in Homewood, Illinois, where Lionberg worked and Schmal had dropped by for a visit during the early morning hours of May 11, 1978. Allegedly, the two captives were driven by the defendants to an abandoned, dilapidated townhouse in East Chicago Heights (subsequently renamed Ford Heights) where the four men repeatedly raped Schmal and fatally shot her and Lionberg.

Adams was sentenced to seventy-five years in prison; Rainge to life in prison without parole; and Williams, to death. Verneal Jimerson, the fourth suspect, was tried and convicted in 1985 and also sentenced to death.

Subsequent DNA testing failed to link the four men to the murders, and they were set free in the summer of 1996 after having spent a combined sixty-five years behind bars. Their story reached a conclusion of sorts on March 5, 1999, when on the recommendation of then-Cook County State's Attorney Dick Devine, the Cook County Board authorized a $36-million payout to the four men and their attorneys to settle charges that Cook County Sheriff's police mishandled the case and engaged in intentional investigative misconduct.

Exoneration of Williams, Rainge, Adams, and Jimerson brought global accolades to Protess and his three former students —Stephanie Goldstein, Stacy Delo, and Laura Sullivan—who had worked on the case as part of a 1996 Protess class project, and to Rene Brown, a private investigator who had been hired in 1980 by the families of Dennis Williams and William Rainge to assist in proving their innocence in the Ford Heights crime.

Put briefly, the Goldstein, Delo, Sullivan contribution to unwinding this apparent injustice was multifold and startling. Sullivan recounted their work in exonerating the four men in an article she penned for the *Baltimore Sun* in June 27, 1999. The account begins with a mid-1996 meeting the three students had with Paula Gray, a key witness in the case. During that tearful encounter in 1996, they obtained a statement from Gray, an illiterate woman with mild cognitive disability, by then thirty-four-years-old, who had implicated the four men in the 1978 murders when she was just seventeen. She told the students, during their visit to her home in a South Side Chicago housing project, that she had "lied" to investigators in 1978 because they told her that if she didn't finger the four defendants, she would spend the rest of her life in jail. In addition, she said that investigators had kept her in a hotel room for three days, cutting her off from her family and community and subjecting her to nearly nonstop interrogation.

The truly damning evidence came several weeks before the Gray interview, however. Sifting through a dozen boxes of case files stacked in a downtown Chicago office building, Goldstein, Delo, and Sullivan discovered an envelope containing informal police notes, known as "street files," in which a police informant named Marvin Simpson had told authorities shortly after the murders, eighteen years before, that he knew who the perpetrators were. In the street files, Simpson identifies the real killers as Arthur "Red" Robinson, Juan "Johnnie" Rodriguez, and Dennis Johnson and his brother Ira Johnson. Inexplicably, Cook County Sheriff investigators never acted on that tip nor did investigators or Cook County prosecutors ever turn the street files over to defense attorneys before, during, or after the 1978 Ford Heights Four trial.

In validation of the three former students' tireless work, Arthur "Red" Robinson, forty-three, entered into an agreement with the Cook County State's Attorney's office and pleaded guilty to his role in the Schmal/Lionberg murders and was sentenced to life in 1997. Two of the others, Johnnie Rodriguez, thirty-seven, and Ira Johnson, also thirty-seven, were convicted earlier that year following separate jury trials and also received life sentences. Dennis Johnson, brother of Ira, had died several years before of a drug overdose.

Basking in the afterglow of the Ford Heights Four win with Protess and the students was Rob Warden, who in 1998 was named executive director of Northwestern University Law School's Center on Wrongful Convictions, which he had cofounded that same year with Lawrence C. Marshall, a Northwestern law faculty member (now a professor at Stanford University Law School). Marshall has long advocated that U.S. law schools have at least one faculty member who is against the death penalty.

Warden had first planted seeds of doubt about the guilt of the Ford Heights Four years before, beginning with an article he co-authored in 1982 in the *Chicago Lawyer*. Headlined, "Will We Execute an Innocent Man? The Dennis Williams Case," the long, detailed report discredited the prosecution, defense counsel, and even the judge in the 1978 trial of Williams, Rainge, and Adams. (Jimerson was tried and convicted separately from the other three.)

The 1996 Ford Heights victory was front-page news in major newspapers and periodicals across the country and even overseas. It was covered by *People* magazine, the *New York Times, Chicago Tonight,* NBC's *Dateline,* ABC News' *Person of the Week,* the *Oprah Winfrey Show,* and more. Literary agents in search of hot new titles and Hollywood producers exploring movie rights all but lined up outside Protess's office in Fisk Hall, a four-story edifice adjacent to the Lake Michigan shoreline and home to the Medill Journalism School since its founding in the 1920s.

Accolades notwithstanding, what should have been an unmitigated triumph diminished significantly after a $1-million Walt Disney Company movie offer about the Ford Heights case triggered nasty infighting between Protess and the three students, plus Rene Brown, the private investigator. Chief issues underlying the dispute, which exploded into the public domain in the fall of 1996, were the questions of who deserved credit for achieving the four men's release, should a movie ever be produced, and, more importantly, how would the pot of gold for the movie rights be divvied up.

A principal origin of Protess's distress in this situation seemed to be the attention and adulation that the media was practically showering on his three former students—white, young, twenty-plus-year-olds from upper-income backgrounds who had ventured into impoverished and dangerous Chicago-area neighborhoods in pursuit of justice. All to the exclusion of their former professor.

On November 10, 1996, Eric Zorn, a *Chicago Tribune* columnist and generally an uncritical supporter of Protess for the professor's work in exposing wrongful prosecutions, wrote a piece about it. "Credit the kids," the Zorn column opened. "They were a storybook team. Stephanie Goldstein, a future law student...was the brains.... Stacy Delo, an aspiring documentary filmmaker... was the heart.... And Laura Sullivan...was the guts; the tough-talking cynic who wouldn't be intimidated by the underclass milieu in which this story was still hidden."

The narrative was somewhat tarnished a few days later in a lengthy piece in the *Chicago Reader* that headlined, "Ford

Heights: Justice and a Piece of the Action." The lengthy column chronicled in detail the rancorous jealousies that had erupted between Protess and his three ex-students and the name-calling that went on between the two camps in the wake of the Disney movie offer.

At one point, the *Reader* article states, Protess and Warden had been waiting months for Goldstein, Delo, and Sullivan to sign on to a package deal that Protess and Warden had worked out with Disney. Hinting that the three former students refused to agree to the Protess/Warden proposal, in part because of mistrust of how the movie would portray their roles should any Hollywood production of the case ever be made, the *Reader* quotes Protess as saying, "If this were a just world, the girls would get nothing and the guys (the four freed prisoners) would get everything. But this isn't a just world or the guys wouldn't be in prison for sixty-five years. As Hollywood defines art, the girls are important to the story. As Rob (Warden) and I see it, the former students are not important."

The feud with the students intensified in September 1996. That was when the three students made an appearance on the *Oprah Winfrey Show*. Protess also had been invited but decided, in his own words, to "boycott" the show because of the media distortions that he felt were developing all around him with regard to the Ford Heights case.

"We're talking now with three college students—Stephanie, Stacy, and Laura—who took on a class assignment and ended up freeing four innocent men from jail," the famed TV talk-show host began. "And I'm thinking now all over Hollywood they're looking at you, and they're thinking of the series they can start... *The Mod Squad* of the '90s, *Charlie's Angels*."

Even Brown, the Ford Heights Four investigator who, as an African-American, played an indispensable role in providing access for the young white students to relevant individuals in troubled black neighborhoods, felt slighted by Protess. His complaint: That Protess belittled his role, often failed to mention his contributions during public addresses about the case, and frequently treated him as some sort of personal valet.

While a Hollywood movie never materialized, the successful campaign to free the four men became the subject of *The Promise of Justice,* an August 1998 book by Protess and Warden. A Missouri native and no newcomer to Chicago's world of journalism, in addition to being a long-time associate of Protess, Warden was a former investigative reporter, foreign correspondent, and editor for the now-defunct *Chicago Daily News* in addition to founding the *Chicago Lawyer.* He was also a political issues consultant and a winner of myriad industry awards for his tireless journalism work.

That book followed an earlier Protess/Warden hardcover titled *Gone in the Night,* a May 1994 account of the legal saga of David Dowaliby and his wife, Cynthia. The couple from Midlothian, Illinois, a suburb southwest of Chicago, was accused in 1988 of abducting Cynthia's seven-year-old biological daughter, Jaclyn, from her bed in the middle of the night and murdering her. Cynthia was directed out of the case during a Cook County jury trial. Though the jury convicted David, the conviction was later reversed on appeal and ended in 1992 when the Illinois Supreme Court declined to review the case. With Protess acting as screenwriter, Warden the consultant, *Gone in the Night* was made into a two-part series aired by CBS in 1996.

In the aftermath of the Ford Heights Four case, Protess and Warden soon found themselves elevated to new roles. In 1998 Warden was named executive director of the just-opened Center on Wrongful Convictions, Bluhm Legal Clinic, Northwestern University School of Law—an entity dedicated to identifying and rectifying wrongful convictions, including those not involving DNA evidence. The following year, Protess was named founding director of the newly created Medill Innocence Project, an initiative launched by Medill faculty to reinvestigate murder convictions in Illinois and determine if people were wrongly convicted and, according to the former professor, to give undergraduate students "firsthand experience in investigating wrongful convictions."

Warden explained that the Center was a direct outgrowth of the first annual Conference on Wrongful Convictions that he cosponsored with Professor Marshall in 1998. In a September 11, 2013, interview with the *National Law Journal*, Warden explained its origins saying, "We brought to a single stage at Northwestern twenty-eight people who had been exonerated and released from death rows around the country. It really was kind of an amazing event. I remember sitting there with my wife, and there was a jam-packed auditorium and people giving a standing ovation to people who had been exonerated in cases where they had been sentenced to death. I thought, 'Hey, we can abolish the death penalty.' And we basically went from there. The Center on Wrongful Convictions was an outgrowth of that conference."

Against this backdrop, Anthony Porter, rather logically, came to be included in the new course developed by Protess. A few days after Labor Day 1998, Protess had received a call from Aviva Futorian, a Chicago lawyer and an advocate of social justice, a veteran of the civil rights struggles of the 1960s, and an unyielding opponent of the death penalty.

A graduate of Brandeis University more than thirty years before, Futorian had participated in the civil rights movement's Freedom Summer in 1964 and beyond, working closely with the Student Nonviolent Coordinating Committee in Holly, Mississippi. She, along with Roy DeBerry, a comrade in the civil rights movement, cofounded the Hill Country Project in Benton County, Mississippi, dedicated to improving education facilities, job training, and job development for the less fortunate. Futorian, who had obtained a law degree, later moved to Chicago where she worked for a time with the Anti-Defamation League before opening a law practice that focused on prisoners' rights and penal reform.

Futorian told Protess that she was calling to seek his assistance in an urgent matter. She said she had been consulting with Dan Sanders, a young, inexperienced attorney representing Porter, who was scheduled for execution on September 23. She added that there were issues surrounding Porter's competency and his guilt. She also said that Sanders, who had been hired by Porter family members for a modest sum, had told her that Offie Green, the mother of Marilyn Green, had signed an affidavit expressing her longtime belief that Porter was innocent of the pool murders. Futorian said Sanders had included the affidavit in his petition to the Illinois Supreme Court in a frantic, last-ditch effort to halt Porter's execution.

According to Futorian, Protess replied he had had been reading about the Porter case and although it sounded interesting, the issue was moot because Porter was to be executed on September 23, five days before his class was scheduled to begin. Just fifty hours before Porter was to be executed, the Illinois Supreme Court granted Sanders's request for a stay—with assists from Aviva Futorian, Lawrence Marshall, and a couple of Marshall's law students—pending the outcome of a competency hearing to be conducted under the auspices of Thomas R. Fitzgerald, Chief Judge of the Cook County Criminal Court. Protess reversed himself and added the Porter case to his new class.

3

Fall 1998 Medill Students Ramp Up

In keeping with the guidelines of his new class, the News Media and Capital Punishment, which launched on September 28, 1998, Protess divided the fall-session students into four teams. With seventeen students enrolled, Protess broke the class down into three teams of four students each and a fourth team consisting of five students.

To meet the new course's objective, the four teams would, at least in theory, spend the three months of the fall quarter reviewing virtually all aspects of the death penalty case that had been assigned to them. From initial police investigations of the case, through the indictments, trials, and sentencing—and everything in between—the goal was to determine whether or not the defendant had received a fair shake. To put it another way, the team wanted to determine if any police, prosecutorial, or judicial errors had taken place during the suspect's journey through the relevant legal system.

Fulfilling his pledge to Aviva Futorian, Protess included the Anthony Porter case in the new course. As noted, Porter's attorney, Dan Sanders—with an assist from others, including Futorian and Marshall—had obtained a stay of execution pending an assessment of the inmate's mental capability. Sanders and the others claimed that the defendant's IQ came in at a surprisingly low 51.[1]

In just a few weeks the decision to include the Porter case would have unimaginable consequences for Cook County State's Attorney Dick Devine; for one of Devine's top deputies; for a couple of young assistant prosecutors in his office, one of whom would go on to become a Cook County criminal court judge; for Porter; and, most profoundly of all, for a former Chicago man who was living in Milwaukee.

The four students assigned to the Porter case were all seniors. The team included a young man named Tom McCann and three young women, Cara Rubinsky, Lori D'Angelo, and Shawn Armbrust. Initially at least, their goal was to talk to psychologists, psychiatrists, and other relevant academics to develop additional evidence to help achieve a single, simple end: to prove Sanders's claim that with an IQ as low as 51, Porter was so mentally challenged that he was not a fit candidate to be put to death.

As McCann, Rubinsky, D'Angelo, Armbrust, and members of the three other teams embarked on their ultimate missions, however, they were given collateral assignments that they were responsible for undertaking as well. Foremost among those collateral assignments, the students were required to attend, discuss, and write a paper about a three-day gathering titled the National Conference on Wrongful Convictions and the Death Penalty.

Hosted by the Northwestern University School of Law at its downtown-Chicago campus, the event took place in mid-November 1998. The first gathering exceeded all expectations, drawing an estimated 1,400 death-penalty opponents, lawyers, ex-death-row inmates, relatives of inmates who had been put to death, and students from all over the country, even a few from overseas.

Speakers included Bianca Jagger; U.S. Representative Jesse Jackson, Jr.; and Samuel Reese Sheppard, the son of Dr. Sam

Sheppard, who, in light of, at that time, recently discovered new evidence, had been wrongfully convicted of murdering his wife in 1954. Robert Meeropol, son of convicted Soviet spies Julius and Ethel Rosenberg, spoke of the emotional turmoil he experienced at the age of six when his parents were executed in 1953. Randall Dale Adams, sentenced to death in 1977 for the murder of a Dallas police officer, was also in attendance. Adams had been exonerated as a result of information uncovered and presented by filmmaker Errol Morris in an acclaimed 1988 documentary, *The Thin Blue Line*. And Barry Scheck, cofounder of the Innocence Project at the Benjamin N. Cardozo School of Law-Yeshiva University in New York, was also there.

"The law is a machine that can cause tremendous hurt," said guest speaker DePaul University law professor Stephan Landsman, offering an observation about the many perils inherent in the U.S. justice system and reflecting a general theme weaving through the conference. "We never talk about that as lawyers and teachers. It's a dangerous machine."

Statistics featured heavily at the 1998 conference. According to participants, seventy-three men and two women had been released from death rows across the country since 1972, usually after many years "on the edge of destruction for crimes they did not commit." To put it another way, for every seven executions since 1972—there had been about 500 up to 1998—one prisoner had been found innocent, declared Northwestern University law professor Marshall, a tireless anti-death-penalty advocate and principal organizer of the conference.

Most prominent among the attendees were twenty-eight exonerated "death prisoners," as the forum referred to them, who provided an emotional highlight to the conference during a culminating plenary session on Saturday night. One at a time, the once-condemned-to-die individuals marched slowly across the stage of the Thorne Auditorium, each with a bright yellow sun-flower in hand that he or she placed in a large vase to symbolize the life that had been spared.

"I don't see how you could look at these flowers that were almost extinguished," Marshall told the tearful audience, "and tell me the death penalty works." One attendee referred to the twenty-eight former inmates seated on stage as "a living graveyard." Others, also fighting back tears, referred to the group as "a stage of honor."

Also seated on the "stage of honor" was Dennis Williams, one of the Ford Heights Four defendants who had been sentenced to death and spent decades on death row for his alleged role in the rape of Carol Schmal and the murder of Schmal and her fiancé, Lawrence Lionberg, following their abduction from a Homewood gas station in 1978.

"My name is Dennis Williams," he said, sitting on a folding chair with the others as he faced the standing-room-only audi-ence. "Had the State of Illinois gotten its way, I'd be dead today." He added that he had become an artist since his 1996 exoneration.

A second man, also from Illinois, was Rolando Cruz, who served on death row after he was twice convicted and sentenced to death for the 1983 rape and murder of ten-year-old Jeanine Nicarico. The case was a notorious miscarriage of justice in DuPage County, Illinois. "I prayed in the morning I would be able to sleep at night. I prayed at night that I would be able to wake up in the morning," he said of his ordeal on death row.

The Medill students also were instructed by their professor to meet with Sanders, Porter's attorney, and Appolon Beaudouin, an investigator for the Illinois Appellate Defenders Office who in the late 1990s was steeped in his own efforts to save Porter from execution. The Office of the State Appellate Defender's principal function is to represent indigent persons on appeal in criminal cases when appointed by the Illinois Supreme Court, the Appellate Court, or the Circuit Court. Together Sanders and Beaudouin provided valuable initial information and leads in the students' efforts.

Beaudouin directed the students to a trove of sworn affidavits, many of them gathered by Kenneth Flaxman, a Chicago attorney who had thrown the anti-death-penalty playbook at both the state and federal courts in the mid- to late-1980s in an effort to get a new trial for Porter. More than a half-dozen Flaxman appeals and other filings—including a request for a writ of certiorari or hearing before the U.S. Supreme Court, based on Flaxman claims ranging from Porter's innocence to ineffective assistance of counsel by Gursel, jury bias, and suppression of exculpatory evidence—were turned away by the courts.

Some of the affidavits Beaudouin gave the students were more than mildly interesting, to be sure. There was, for example, the affidavit signed by Joyce Heywood on April 4, 1992, ten years after the pool murders. In that four-page document, she stated she knew a man by the name of Alstory Simon and his wife, Inez; that she knew the victims, Marilyn Green and Jerry Hillard; and that there were increasingly bad feelings between Alstory Simon and Hillard who was selling drugs for Simon and withholding money from him. Following the pool shootings, Heywood said she asked Inez's son, Sonny Jackson, if he knew who the real killer was.

Sonny Jackson's response was, "Why should I answer you because you already know," Heywood stated in her affidavit.

"I said let me put it another way. Did Al[story] do this? Sonny told me that Al killed them," her affidavit concluded.

Another fascinating document was the April 7, 1992, affidavit of Ricky Young. "Alstory Simon, who we called Al, is a drug supplier. Jerry Hillard was selling drugs for Al. I was at 5323 S. Federal, Apartment #705, the Robert Taylor Homes, when I overheard a conversation that Al was having with other people. I could tell

Al was upset, but he wasn't showing it. Al was talking about how Jerry and the girl were taken care of."

Other affidavits fell into the "plain foolish" category. One example was that of Tanya Mardis, who signed a two-page affidavit on May 19, 1988. "While I was talking with Jerry and Marilyn, we were joined by a woman named Inez and her boyfriend. I saw Inez whisper into Marilyn's ear and I then saw Marilyn say something to Jerry. I could not hear what Inez whispered to Marilyn and I could not hear what Marilyn said to Jerry.... About three and perhaps five minutes after Inez joined us, I left to go upstairs to my mother's apartment to use the washroom. At that time, I was in the ninth month of pregnancy and I had to use the washroom frequently."

Another damning affidavit must have grabbed the students' attention as well. That is the April 23, 1987, affidavit signed by Offie Green, Marilyn Green's mother. In it, she asserts that Inez and her "boyfriend"—presumably Alstory Simon, whom she does not identify by name—went to the park with Marilyn and Jerry and that Marilyn had received her welfare check that day and had cashed it. She adds that, in her opinion, Marilyn and Jerry were lured into the park by Inez and "her boyfriend" as part of a plot "to set her up" and rob Marilyn of her welfare money. "In several conversations with Chicago police officers after August 16, 1982, I asked what the police had found out about Inez. I told the officers that I didn't think that Tony [Anthony] Porter was shot (sic) Marilyn and Jerry. Each time that I asked about Inez, the officers told me that I should not worry about the investigation and that the police were certain that Tony Porter was guilty."

As mentioned, early in their review, McCann, D'Angelo, Armbrust, and Rubinsky had focused their efforts on proving what had led the Illinois Supreme Court to delay, at least temporarily, Porter's execution in the first instance. That was to prove, as

Sanders had alleged in his petition to the state high court, that Porter was so mentally deficient that he was an unfit candidate for death. For example, in November Shawn Armbrust sent a memo detailing an interview she had with the Reverend Ira Banks, death-row chaplain at Menard Correctional Center in Chester, Illinois, where Porter was being held at the time. In her telephone interview with Banks, the student is still focusing on the prisoner's mental state: "Banks said that he occasionally thought Porter did understand his punishment, but mostly did not, because Porter is so unstable and confused about very simple matters.... Banks passes out cards for various holidays that inmates can send to their children and families.... He said Porter never knew his children's names or ages, and he had the same problem with him every holiday for four years."

However, in the wake of the affidavits and other interviews, the students engaged in a powerful mid-course correction in which they shifted their efforts beyond proving Porter's mental frailty to proving his innocence and perhaps even determining, before their senior year was over, who the real pool triggerman was— just like their predecessor students in the Ford Heights Four case.

That pivot occurred sometime in early November, as evidenced by a November 5 e-mail sent by Protess to Paul Ciolino, a licensed and frequently armed private investigator who was assisting the professor and his students, particularly with critical interviews and tracking down individuals the students needed to talk to but were having difficulty locating.

"Hey Paul," the Protess e-mail begins, "now it's your turn to find people. Here's what I have on the guy we're almost certain was the killer in the crime for which Anthony Porter faces death. Alstroy (sic) Simon, DOB 06/02/50 last known address (1991) 1312 W. Cottage Place, Milwaukee... He was convicted of armed robbery in Cook County and released by IDOC shortly before the armed robbery/double homicide that led to Porter's arrest. Simon and his girlfriend Inez Jackson (no other identifying info) were last seen with the victims before they were killed."

There is the November 11, 1998, memo as well, from Armbrust, McCann, D'Angelo, and Rubinsky bearing the title, "Washington Park re-enactment," with attachments described as, "Park diagram and summary of William Taylor and Henry Williams's account of their actions the night of the crimes." According to the memo, the students' visit to the pool in Washington Park, which was accompanied by a WBBM-TV Channel Two film crew, and their re-enactment of the crime raised "a few possible discrepancies and areas for further investigation we noted during the re-enactment."

One such discrepancy? "Taylor said he saw a gun in the suspect's left hand as he [Porter] ran by. A member of our group ran by the south end of the pool with an object in her hand, which we had trouble identifying in broad daylight after she had run past. In addition, Taylor said the suspect had the gun in his left hand... we should check whether Porter is left- or right-handed."

A December 7, 1998, detailed memo to Protess from the four students also makes it clear how their investigative trail had gone from proving Porter's mental deficiency to proving the defendant's innocence. "We began investigating the Anthony Porter case in early October," the students' memo begins. "Unlike other groups in our class, our investigation began on the issue of Porter's competency to be executed rather than on the issue of his innocence."

The memo continues, "Consequently, most of our earlier activities and findings relate to competency, and the later findings relate more to his innocence. We worked with Porter's attorney and the Appellate Defenders Office. In the course of our work, we found a great deal of evidence to support both Porter's incompetency to be executed and his possible innocence. The next students to investigate the case should have more time to investigate innocence issues, and we think they will develop more evidence that proves Anthony Porter's innocence."

By early December, with the Medill team all but certain they had the true killer in their sights, something of an enigmatic episode took place. With Protess at the wheel of his car and Armbrust, a native of Brookfield, Wisconsin, and Rubinsky, of Pittsburgh, Pennsylvania, riding along, the trio set out for Alstory Simon's Milwaukee home, a brick bungalow at 213 E. Wright Street, about 5 p.m. on December 9.

With Protess waiting in his car across the street from the house, the students knocked on the door and were told by an unidentified woman that Simon was still at work but would be home at 7 p.m. The three returned to Wright Street two hours later, and with Protess again waiting outside in his parked car, the students rang the doorbell. When Simon opened the front door, they told him that they were students who were working on a "class project," a long-ago criminal case that took place in Chicago.

Simon invited them in, and in response to several of the students' inquiries, he gave answers that seemed to contradict the case the students had been building. Simon said he had been "good friends" with Hillard and Green, the couple had been planning their wedding at the time, and that the double homicide "was very painful" for him. But, he added, with the passage of time he "had managed to block it out" and get on with his life.

Yes, he and his wife, Inez, had been with the victims the night of the Bud Billiken Parade, but as they strolled into Washington Park and spotted a group of ominous looking men, Simon and Inez peeled off, stopping for ice cream before returning home to the kids. Before parting company, Simon said he warned Hillard and Green not to go into the park because it was dangerous. Finally, Simon said he had been "worried about Jerry, because Jerry was getting involved in some bad things."

Rubinsky said the interview lasted about twenty minutes and that when it concluded, the two students and Simon exited his home and walked toward Protess, still in his car across the street. Protess jumped out and, ordering the students to step aside out of earshot, had a brief conversation with Simon. What Protess said to Simon is not known, but he did give Simon his business card and asked Simon to call him.

A month later, when asked why Protess pulled Simon out of earshot of the students, Rubinsky said, "I think the professor asked us to walk away at the end for a minute...but I don't think he [Protess] said anything. I think he wanted to make eye contact—tried to make eye contact with Alstory."

The memo notwithstanding, Tom McCann, who had taken a de facto lead in directing the four-person team, was not about to wait for the winter quarter to begin the task of proving Porter's innocence. Just four days later, on December 11, 1998, McCann and Ciolino drove to an apartment building at 4128 N. Clarendon Avenue, where William Taylor lived. Taylor, it is recalled, was one of a pair of star witnesses who, testifying for the State in 1983, told jurors that he was in the pool on August 15, 1982, and that he saw Anthony Porter shoot his victims and flee from the pool, passing so close to Taylor that Taylor, who knew Porter from the neighborhood, got a good look at his face.

McCann already had talked to Taylor once before on the phone, on November 14, after McCann had obtained his telephone number from Beaudouin, the Appellate Defender investigator. Beaudouin told McCann that he had obtained an affidavit from Taylor during a visit to Taylor's apartment in August 1997, in which he got Taylor to assert that police had threatened him and held him overnight in a jail cell without charging him the day following the August 15 pool murders.

When McCann called Taylor on November 14 to discuss the affidavit, however, Taylor expressed frustration at being hassled by calls from the likes of McCann, calls and visits by Beaudouin and others, all wanting him to change his trial testimony. Taylor told McCann his mother had been sick and had recently died, and he was under a lot of stress.

Then, Taylor volunteered a bombshell utterance that McCann memorialized in a memo. "There is no doubt in my mind that this man [Porter] is guilty," Taylor told McCann. "I will not be happy until Porter is finally executed." McCann added in his memo, "He [Taylor] sounded bothered and not happy to talk about the Porter case, but I agree with Appolon [Beaudouin] that he will talk if you keep pushing him."

And McCann and Ciolino did keep pushing during their December 11, 1998, visit to Taylor's apartment building. Finding Taylor not at home, the two lingered in the building's ground floor lobby until between 7 and 8 P.M. when Taylor arrived. With Ciolino playing the bad cop, and McCann the good cop—an interviewing technique that Protess taught his students as part of the fall-quarter class—they confronted Taylor.

After introducing themselves, Ciolino explained why they wanted to talk to him.

"I have something to tell you, William," Ciolino told Taylor. "It is not going to go away. We have to talk about this sooner or later. There is a competency hearing coming up, and there are issues about his [Porter's] innocence. And he is going to be put to death pretty soon, so whether you cooperate or not, you are going to have to deal with this sometime."

About twenty minutes later, a beleaguered Taylor, who had said more than once that his life never was the same following the

1983 Porter trial and that he would not rest until Porter was executed, signed an affidavit that Ciolino had written out in longhand in the hotel lobby. Ciolino, also a Notary Public, added his signature, as did McCann, the witness.

Dated December 11, 1998, the affidavit asserted that Taylor was in the park the night of the shootings, did not see Porter shoot anyone, never saw Porter with a gun, and did not see who shot the victims that day.

However, try as McCann and Ciolino might, they could not get the witness to say also that he had not seen Porter in the pool area the night of the shootings. So instead they omitted from his affidavit the attestation that he had in fact seen Porter there.

One of the more curious, never-explained episodes of the Porter narrative occurred just four days after Ciolino and McCann had obtained their affidavit. On December 14, Ciolino and this time Protess returned to Taylor's Clarendon residence, picked him up, and drove him to Ann Sather's, a popular eatery not far from where Taylor lived. There, after plying Taylor with wine, they asked him—and he complied—to sign a second affidavit, witnessed by Protess and notarized by Ciolino. The December 14 affidavit is a "mirror image" of the December 11 affidavit, Protess later would agree without explaining why the second affidavit was needed.

On December 16, as part of an exclusive story Protess had promised producers at WBBM-TV Channel Two in Chicago, Protess picked up Taylor at his apartment on Clarendon around 4 P.M. and drove him to the station's studio on McClurg Court in Chicago. There during the 6 P.M. and 10 P.M. television newscasts, Taylor read his watered-down affidavit to WBBM's viewers, word for word.

The Taylor appearance on the December 16 WBBM-TV news raised eyebrows among viewers and fellow members of Chicago's competing news outlets alike. It also represented the first step by Protess and his students in engineering the gradual, ultimately successful erosion and reversal of a criminal case in which police in 1982 had arrested the right man; a jury, after hearing all the evidence in 1983, had convicted the right man; and a judge, following a post-conviction hearing, had rightfully sentenced the defendant to death.

I   Approximately 2.2 percent of the population have an IQ (intelligence quotient) below 70, which is the threshold number of what used to be referred to as "retardation." An IQ rating between 50 and 70 is called "mild mental deficiency," what once was called "educable mentally handicapped." A score between 35 and 50 was called "moderate mental retardation." So the IQ number that was ascribed to Porter essentially indicated that his cognitive ability was very low.

4

The December 16 Jail Visit and Beyond

On December 16, 1998, Protess, McCann, Armbrust, Rubinsky, and Dan Sanders visited the defendant in Cook County Jail at 2854 W. 31st Street in Chicago. Clad in a beige jumpsuit, his ankles and wrists shackled, Porter was seated in a small room in Division Nine of the sprawling county jail complex. Division Nine is a twin-block, three-story structure that houses more than a thousand of humankind's most violent malefactors. This is where they found Porter.

Porter had escaped execution by mere hours the previous September, when the Illinois Supreme Court acted on the emergency petition filed by Sanders, Marshall, et al. He was returned to Cook County Jail, and a competency hearing was scheduled to begin by the end of the following January before Thomas R. Fitzgerald, chief judge of the Cook County Criminal Courts.

Protess, McCann, Rubinsky, and Armbrust had never met Porter before. The December 16 meeting presented an excellent opportunity for the journalism students and their professor to confront Porter with some very hard questions, to behave like the investigative journalists the course was supposedly training them to be. They had the opportunity to get to the bottom of the pool murders once and for all. The list of potential interview questions and follow-up subjects was long.

Were you in the pool area that night, Anthony? How is it the State, at the time of the killings, had no fewer than six witnesses putting you in the pool area? Why didn't you take the stand in your own defense? Of course you are under no obligation to do so, but you're facing the death penalty, so why not?

And Fat Luke, your most important alibi witness—he was the best you could come up with? He told the jury that you and he and a couple of others were smoking weed, drinking Wild Irish Rose, and talking about the old times in a play lot in the Robert Taylor Homes at the time of the killings. And then, under cross-examination, Fat Luke told jurors he was a low-level member of the Cobra Stones street gang who would commit murder if ordered to do so by gang higher-ups. And he admitted under cross-examination to having told police a year earlier that he was home asleep in bed when the murders took place, not with you and the others in a Robert Taylor Homes play lot.

And what can you tell us about your own violent past? How about Earl Lewis? Can you tell us you didn't kick his dog and then shoot Lewis in the head after he objected? Tell us that—even though you pleaded guilty to that shooting and got six years for it. And how about Douglas McGhee? He said you were in the bleachers next to the pool, which was filled with swimmers, under a sun-drenched sky when you beat him senseless and took his $800. What about that? What about Chicago police officer Anthony Liace, one of the first responders to the 1982 shootings, who said he stopped and frisked you as you were racing from the murder scene?

With all of these possible questions hanging out there for the journalism students to posit, what is the first question McCann asks the prisoner whose case he and the other students have been investigating practically 24/7 for the previous three months?

"How are they treating you in here?"

And the second McCann question?

"How is the food?"

At one point McCann does ask a relevant question, but it is never followed up.

"You know there is someone…in the testimony there is a police officer that said he stopped you and frisked you in the park," McCann tells Porter. "You know, just come clean, you know, if they did see you there and you didn't have a gun, that's good for you. You know, so if you really were that person, tell us and it might help you out."

Porter responded that he was not in the pool or the park that night; he was in the Robert Taylor Homes play lot.

Rubinsky would later admit that she did not discuss Porter's alibi with him during the visit because she did not know what his alibi was, even though she had been researching the Porter case for more than four months. Instead, she said she "just spoke with him, just 'how are you doing? Hello.' That was it."

And Armbrust? What did she ask the convicted murderer as metal jail doors clanked open and shut up and down the hallway outside their small interviewing room?

"I asked how his headaches were. Because he gets very bad headaches."

The meaningless exchanges between the students and the prisoner, which lasted for about ninety minutes, suggest a central fact acknowledged by Armbrust under oath during an appearance she made before a Cook County grand jury just two month later. She described the team's thinking at the time of their December jail visit as, "We were convinced that there was no case against him on December 11 when William Taylor recanted his testimony.… I guess when we met him we were convinced that he was innocent."

As it turned out, however, the jail visit was by no means an empty exercise. To put it another way, Porter had prepared for the meeting and was able to give his listeners precisely what they were seeking—a pair of explosive new investigative leads that, if pursued, would take them to the "real" killer and exonerate Porter.

"Alstory Simon was the guy" the students had to get, the shackled prisoner declared to his visitors. "Because he had done the crime."

Again and again Porter said he was innocent, and if the students wanted to solve the murders and prove his innocence, they had to find Inez Jackson, Alstory Simon's estranged wife, and Jackson's nephew, Walter Jackson. If they got ahold of Inez and Walter, they would tell the students who the real pool killer was.

When the interview was finished, Porter expressed his gratitude for his audience's "willingness to investigate his claims of innocence." He then "hugged" each member of the group before being led back to his Division Nine cell by Cook County sheriff's deputies.

The Medill team departed the Cook County Jail surely feeling a degree of exhilaration. They had hit one over the fence. The two solid tips, once tracked down, would lead them to the truth.

Locating Walter and interviewing him would be simple enough, because the students were told that he was incarcerated in the Illinois Department of Corrections facility in downstate Danville, serving a long stretch for first-degree murder. Finding Inez, on the other hand, presented a challenge. Estranged from her husband, and having surrendered long before to alcohol and drugs and then prostitution to support those addictions, Inez had disappeared into that netherworld and could be almost anywhere. As they departed the jail that early December day, the only thing the students knew about Inez was that she was living somewhere in Milwaukee.

The student group broke for the Christmas holidays, and

though the Porter investigation did not formally begin again until the first day of the winter quarter, Armbrust did not remain idle. Living with her family in Brookfield, a suburb of Milwaukee, population 37,000, with a 1.2 percent black population and a median household income above $85,000, she spent much of her winter break scouring County of Milwaukee public records in an effort to find Inez's address.

Real estate, circuit court, building department, and other public records all failed to yield the address of Inez Jackson. Armbrust and her teenage brother, a freshman at Northwestern, also scouted out Alstory Simon's Milwaukee home, driving by it several times in an unsuccessful effort to catch a glimpse of him.

When the first day of the winter quarter began on January 4, 1999, the review of the Porter conviction resumed in earnest, but under slightly altered circumstances. Three of the original fall quarter team members—Tom McCann, Cara Rubinsky, and Shawn Armbrust—were now enrolled in Protess's Investigative Journalism class and were given the green light by their professor to continue their review of Porter's case as their sole assignment in the new class.

The three veteran students were also joined by two newcomers, Syandene Rhodes-Pitts and Erica LaBorgne, who like the others were seniors but unlike them did not have a clue about the Porter case. They replaced Lori D'Angelo, who had opted not to enroll in the Investigative Journalism class.

Recalling Porter's words about talking to the incarcerated Walter Jackson if they wanted to get Simon, Armbrust and the two student newcomers made an initial trip to Danville on January 8, 1999, to interview Jackson and learn from him where they might find Inez, his aunt. No one knew it at the time, but Inez was soon to be diagnosed with the AIDS virus. During a two-hour meeting in a small barren room in the Danville Correctional Facility, the prisoner provided the three students with the names of nearly a dozen friends and relatives of Inez who might be able to lead them to her.

What the students did not know at the time was that Protess and Walter Jackson had had a dark and complex phone conversation over the Christmas holidays. According to court records, Protess had written a letter to Jackson sometime in early to mid-December asking the inmate to call him at his Evanston home, which Jackson did. During that telephone conversation, according to court records, "Protess told Walter Jackson that if Jackson helped Protess free Anthony Porter, that Protess would in turn help Jackson get out of jail."

Protess also told Jackson that he would help Sonny Jackson, Inez's son, get out of a state prison in Stanley, Wisconsin, where he was serving a long sentence for murder. According to court records, Protess, in return for getting the two men out of prison, "wanted Jackson to help him get the cooperation of his aunt, Inez Jackson Simon."

Protess also told Jackson that there would be money waiting for him when he got out of jail. Jackson told Protess he would do whatever Protess wanted.[1]

Subsequently, Jackson called Inez, explained the December conversation he had had with Protess, and told Inez to admit she witnessed Simon shoot the two victims and describe how the shooting took place. If Inez did that, Jackson said Protess promised to get Sonny Jackson out of prison. Inez agreed.

Beyond the Protess promises, Jackson had another motive for signing the affidavit and helping Porter out—a motive completely unknown to the students. Walter Jackson and Anthony Porter had been incarcerated together in Danville in 1994, and during that stretch Porter saved Jackson from getting "shanked," that is stabbed, by a fellow inmate during a violent altercation in the prison yard. Jackson was thankful for the intervention by Porter, and now Jackson wanted to return the favor.

On January 20, Armbrust and LaBorgne made a second trip to the prison to meet with Jackson, this time without Rhodes-Pitts, bearing a typed affidavit that had been prepared by Protess.[11] In the affidavit, which Jackson signed during the January 20 visit and Armbrust and LaBorgne witnessed with their affixed signatures, Jackson asserted that after "seventeen years of silence" his conscience had gotten the better of him, and he was now prepared to testify that Alstory Simon had confessed on the night of the murders that he, Simon, had shot and killed Hillard and Green.

Jackson asserts in his affidavit that several hours after the pool murders, "in the middle of the night, Alstory returned to the apartment. In the presence of myself and Sonny Jackson, Alstory stated that he 'has taken care of' Jerry and Marilyn. He [Alstory] went on to state that he had shot Jerry twice by the bleachers in Washington Park with a .38-caliber blue snub-nose revolver and then had shot Marilyn twice with the same weapon. He did not describe Inez's role in the murders."

That was not all. Jackson submitted a second handwritten affidavit, dated February 4, 1999, just over five pages long. While it is duplicative in parts of his January 20 statement, it asserts that, "The night of the murders, Al got dressed in a jogging suit and left. Al was 'spooky' and 'real quiet.' Al always had a gun. He took his pouch that he kept his gun in with him when he left that night."

The motive for the shootings according to Jackson in his February 4 affidavit?

"Jerry was selling drugs for Alstory. Al was mad at Jerry because Jerry took some drugs and didn't give Al the money for them. Over a two-week period before the murders, I knew that Al was growing more angry (sic) at Jerry for this."

The Medill team now had two of their own affidavits in hand,

Taylor's and Jackson's, and increasingly the Chicago media was taking notice of the group and its accomplishments and reporting them, thanks in large part to Protess's nonstop, behind-the-scenes working of outlets like WBBM-TV Channel Two in Chicago.[III] But the dramatic next stage of the unfolding drama would be engineered primarily by an investigator named Paul Ciolino.

Ciolino, who was working closely with the Medill team, was a private investigator licensed by the State of Illinois, authorized to carry a concealed weapon, and owner of Paul J. Ciolino & Associates, 900 W. Jackson Boulevard in Chicago. On its website Ciolino & Associates claims credit for freeing five individuals from death row, including the Ford Heights Four, and another three from life sentences, all of whom were wrongfully convicted.

"If you are innocent and you are sitting in a jail cell somewhere, there is nothing that we can say to ease your burden," the website text asserts. "However, there is plenty that we can do to regain your freedom. At Paul J. Ciolino & Associates we are the number one agency in the world in regaining the freedom of people who were wrongfully sent to death for a crime in which they were innocent."

A 1974 graduate of Reavis High School in Burbank, Illinois, Ciolino served a four-year hitch in the U.S. Army, where he was a military policeman, achieving the rank of sergeant by the time he was discharged in the early 1980s. An on-again, off-again student at nearly a dozen colleges, while in the service and afterward, Ciolino finally received an associate degree from Moraine Valley Community College in Palos Hills, Illinois, and took his first job as a private investigator for the Loop-headquartered Metro Probe Inc. in 1981.

After two years, he left Metro Probe and opened Illinois Security Services Inc. with Mel Gossmeyer, locating the agency at 29 S. LaSalle Street, Chicago, and providing security guards for area companies. During that time, he also worked for the Illinois Department of Children and Family Services, supervising child-abuse cases.

Finally, in 1987, he founded Paul J. Ciolino & Associates. Ciolino described himself as a close friend of Protess and Warden, both of whom he first met in 1984 when Warden was publisher of *Chicago Lawyer* magazine and Protess was writing for the monthly publication.

Ciolino's loose association with a leading institution of higher learning remains a minor puzzle because the investigator was known to get his hands dirty. Ciolino employed aggressive tactics while pursuing clients' work. When necessary, he "bull-rushed" suspects into confessions. And, again when circumstances necessitated it, he packed a gun and threatened to use it.

As an example of his tactics, in 1994 when the Illinois Department of Professional Regulation fined Ciolino $2,000 and placed him on probation from February 1995 to March 29, 1996. Ciolino caught the complaint for "acting as a private detective without a license," in a case in which he collected a $2,000 fee in exchange for locating a mother who had been hiding.

And there was an incident in July of 2000, in which he was accused in court documents of "knowingly threatening the life" of a Summit man—and the lives of his wife and children—who was engaged in legal wrangling with a Ciolino client. In a surprise visit by Ciolino to the man's south-suburban home, the victim's daughter stated in a court affidavit that on July 9, 2000, about 1 P.M., while watching television with her father, she heard "the doorbell ringing repeatedly and pounding on the door." When her father opened the door, Ciolino was standing there, promising her father he would "end up with a bullet in his head," the daughter alleged.

When asked how it was that a detective with a questionable

professional background, with no official affiliation with a school like Northwestern University, became involved in a Medill Journalism School class project, Protess responded, "I called him and asked for help in locating certain people because he has expertise that we do not have through database searches and that he can do credit checks and the like." Protess emphasized that his sleuth was working for free.

In the end, Ciolino played a role in the Medill investigation that included far more than doing database searches, credit checks, "and the like."

I   December 2005, Second Petition for Post-Conviction Relief filed by Attorneys Terry Ekl and James Sotos.

II   Ibid.

III February 22, 1999, Cook County grand jury testimony of Shawn Armbrust.

5

The Inez Jackson and Alstory Simon Confessions

With William Taylor's and Walter Jackson's affidavits now in hand, the next mission for the Medill students was to locate Inez and obtain a signed affidavit from her. Armbrust and Rhodes-Pitts returned to Milwaukee, and after scouring more public documents they discovered that Inez Simon's birth name was in fact Margaret. With that new information, they located a niece who in turn supplied them with Margaret's home address. They had found her at last.

On January 27, Armbrust and Rubinsky drove to Milwaukee a second time and made an initial contact with Inez at her home. There were about seven other people present, including Inez's daughter Tiffany Jackson. Although Protess and Ciolino were to have accompanied the two students on their first visit with Inez, the professor and Ciolino backed off at the last minute, with the professor telling the students: "We [Ciolino and Protess] decided that it makes the most sense for as many of you as possible to go to Milwaukee tomorrow—without us, at first—to continue the search for Margaret/Inez. We have confidence that you can do it [meet with Inez] on your own, and that we wouldn't add a lot to what needs to be done."

Besides, Protess had more important things to take care of just then. Rather than meet with Inez in Milwaukee, he had to get the Chicago press ready for the explosive news segments that were in the offing. As Protess put it in an e-mail: "I want to spend a good part of the day massaging the media for what's coming during the next week." What he expected was a videotaped confession from Inez, which he was confident he would have in a matter of days.

Without disclosing they had met with Walter Jackson and obtained his affidavit, and without discussing the Porter case, as Protess had instructed them, Armbrust and Rubinsky arranged for Inez to meet Protess in person in the next day or two. The professor told the students to tell Inez that he wanted to give Inez "a message" from Walter Jackson, her nephew. It was a ploy for Protess to get his foot in the door and reaffirm Protess's agreed-upon plan with Jackson: Namely, that Inez had agreed to help Protess in return for the professor's help in freeing Walter from prison.

The ruse worked. Two days later, on January 29, Protess, Armbrust, Rubinsky, and Ciolino drove again to Milwaukee to meet Inez, "who was very sick and very poor and very malnourished"[1] at Inez's home. The all-day meeting started at her house, moved to a German restaurant in the city's central business district, and ended at Armbrust's parents' home in nearby Brookfield. Armbrust's parents were away, her mother vacationing in Florida, her father on business in Australia.

The visitors' overriding goal was to obtain a signed affidavit from Inez accusing her husband, Alstory Simon, of committing the murders and then getting her to repeat that claim on a video that would be shot by Ciolino. Once the affidavit and the video footage were obtained, they would be passed off to Joe Mondello, the CBS WBBM-TV Channel Two producer back in Chicago who, working in concert with Protess for months, was ready to beam the Inez Simon confession to the station's Midwest audience—and provide the video to interested sister stations across the country.

When the crew arrived at Inez's house, about a mile from Alstory's, the first thought that came to Ciolino's mind was to get out of the house and its deplorable surroundings as quickly as possible. Inez appeared to be living the life of "an indentured servant," now infected with HIV, strung out on drugs, and in effect imprisoned in a makeshift apartment in the basement of the residence. To make matters worse, he said there was a passel of disruptive, noisy teenagers playing video games.

Ciolino recalled the Inez encounter this way:

"Inez said, 'You want to talk here?' And I didn't want to talk there. Number one, it was like ninety degrees in the house. It was just miserable in there. There's ten kids in the house, teenagers. I said, 'No.' I said, 'How about if we buy you lunch?' And I mean she was out that door like greased lightning."

So was Ciolino, along with the other members of the team. The visitors took Inez to the first "nice" restaurant they came across—a German restaurant in downtown Milwaukee—where the team and Inez took their seats at a corner booth. Following introductions all around, Inez ordered a bowl of chili and a Budweiser, and with Inez the only one eating or drinking, Ciolino commenced the interview.

"I said, 'Listen, I want you to tell me what you know about this murder that happened with Marilyn and Jerry.' And I mean it came pouring out of her. It was easy."

Following lunch and after obtaining the signed affidavit, en route to the Armbrust home in Brookfield for the video session, the group stopped at a small grocery store "to pick up a couple of things" for the weak, emaciated, and malnourished Inez. Items included "some fruit, some liver, some fruit juice, and a little bit of stuff to make a salad." Also purchased for Inez was a small electric space heater, costing $22, because the woman had complained to her guests that her basement apartment was cold. Protess paid for the food and heater.

Armbrust, Protess, Ciolino, Rubinsky, and Inez Jackson then traveled to the Armbrust home where Inez Jackson sat at the family dining room table. Ciolino unpacked his video gear and set it up, and with the videotape rolling, Inez gave her confession—the one she had bottled up for so many years, a confession that would be broadcast widely and would ultimately spring Porter from death row.

In the video, the feeble-appearing woman alleges that on the night of the shootings, she was in Washington Park with Simon and the two victims, seated in the bleachers, drinking beer. An argument broke out over Hillard withholding drug sales money from Simon. Alstory pulled out a gun, she says, and shot Hillard and Green before grabbing Inez by the arm and pulling her out of the park. After Simon shot and killed her best friend of many years, she asserts on the video, she and her husband stopped for ice cream before going home.

Ciolino explained that Inez had kept the information inside her since 1982 because she feared retribution by her husband and by the Chicago police and the Cook County state's attorney were she to tell the truth. But Inez ultimately acceded to the interview after Ciolino assured her that Martin Abrams, a Chicago attorney who shared offices with Ciolino, would represent her for free should any legal issues arise in connection with her taped confession.

When asked why a Chicago attorney would represent pro bono a destitute prostitute and drug addict afflicted with the AIDS virus and living in Milwaukee in a case involving a nearly twenty-year-old, double-homicide, Ciolino replied, "Because I asked him to do it. Because I do all kinds of stuff free for him. He's one of my tenants and he's always putting the arm on me for free stuff. So once in a while, he's going to have to do something" for free.[11]

In October 2011, Abrams admitted that he rented office space from Ciolino and provided this explanation to the Attorney Registration and Disciplinary Commission, a division of the Illinois Supreme Court, as to why he would travel from Chicago to Milwaukee to represent free of charge a woman in Inez's circumstances:

"I represented Inez pro bono as I believed Inez was not a guilty party and would cooperate with the State. In a phone conversation where she called me, Inez told me she wanted to do the right thing, that Porter did not commit the killings, and she wanted to make it right.... I never expected to be paid for representing her."

Armbrust said the videotape, along with the affidavit signed by the sick woman, subsequently were hand-delivered to producer Joe Mondello at WBBM-TV news and Mike Flannery, a veteran reporter at the station.[111] Flannery and Mondello had been regularly airing the investigative claims of Protess and his students seemingly without determining the merits of those claims. Not to be outdone, other Chicago news outlets—and on occasion, national news organizations—were following their lead.

For Mondello and Flannery, the Ciolino video of Inez laying all the blame on her former husband, together with Inez's affidavit, would be terrific material for Channel Two's next installment, airing that night, January 29, 1999, at approximately 6:11 P.M.

Inez's television address and her affidavit mirrored what Walter Jackson had alleged—namely, she and Alstory and the victims entered the pool area, scaled the bleachers, and took their seats when Alstory and Jerry "started arguing about money that Jerry had stolen from Alstory.... All of a sudden I heard two gunshots. I was shocked. I couldn't believe it." She said Alstory grabbed her by the arm and ripped her from the bleachers before they made their escape.

Inez's televised, videotaped confession was a blockbuster of a scoop for CBS Channel Two, but it would pale in comparison to what was in the offing. When that next installment was aired by Channel Two just five days following, it was destined to do three things: shake the Cook County State's Attorney's Office and the County's judicial system to their cores, plunge members of the Midwest media into a wild feeding frenzy, and stretch human reasoning to the snapping point.

Minutes after the sun came up on February 3, 1999, a Wednesday, five days after an emaciated, weakened Inez Jackson had recorded her video from Brookfield, Wisconsin, Alstory Simon, naked from the waist up, began nodding off, exhausted from a night of snorting cocaine and drinking booze in his home in Milwaukee with his girlfriend Pearl Russ.

Barely conscious, Simon was awakened from his stupor about 6:30 A.M. by two men armed with guns who identified themselves as "police investigators" from Illinois. They accused Simon of having murdered two individuals years earlier in the pool area of Chicago's Washington Park.

The uninvited guests—Paul Ciolino and his assistant, Arnold Reed—told Simon that Inez "and other witnesses" had signed statements alleging that Simon had indeed committed the murders. Despite protestations from Simon that the two men were "crazy" and that they leave his house at once, Simon said the two so-called police investigators from Chicago then slapped a video into a portable player.

As the tape rolled, a black male appeared on the screen, claiming to have been a witness to the 1982 Washington Park slayings of Marilyn Green and Jerry Hillard. The unidentified man—who much later would be revealed as an actor hired and scripted by Ciolino—said Simon was the triggerman.

Simon's intruders had another persuasive trick to play. After showing the video and producing a copy of Inez's signed affidavit and that of Walter Jackson also incriminating Simon, Ciolino did the seemingly impossible. The private eye glanced into a mirror hanging on Simon's wall and by apparent coincidence spotted a news report flashing across Simon's TV, which otherwise was not within sight. He signaled Simon to get out of his chair and watch the newscast.

The TV was tuned to Milwaukee's Channel 50, a locally owned CBS station, and it was rebroadcasting the January 29 story in which Inez is seen and heard asserting that Simon had committed the murders. There on the screen was the gaunt-looking Inez stating she saw Simon shoot the victims, Inez's affidavit alleging the same, and breakaways featuring still photos of Protess, the bearded choreographer who had coordinated Ciolino's visit with the Milwaukee broadcast.

Ciolino described Simon's reaction to the newscast this way:

"And I looked into a mirror on the wall and I seen (sic) the beginning of the CBS network story that had been on the previous evening news. They were playing it again. This is about 7:30 or 7:40 A.M. And me and Alstory walked over to the TV and there was the whole story, about three-and-a-half minutes of why Alstory Simon committed the murder on network news. And Alstory is sitting there watching it and he's staring at it and he's listening to the whole thing. So everything that I just told him about the media, he's seeing it for himself now. And I had no idea this was on. He had no idea it was coming on. It just happened."[IV]

The surreal events unfolding around Simon that morning in his own home triggered a well of fear within. "Ciolino kept telling me that they had all the evidence they needed to convict me," Alstory later attested. "That I was going to go down for these murders and end up on death row, and there was nothing I could do about it. After seeing this story on the TV, I was no longer just angry. I was scared to death. For the first time, I believed that I was actually going to be charged with committing the murders," Simon stated in a sworn affidavit.

Ciolino told Simon that all Protess wanted was to free Porter, that when Porter got out, millions of dollars would be flying around from book deals, Hollywood movies, and the like. And Simon would be sharing in the bounty. Simon had to move quickly, however, because Chicago police were on their way to Milwaukee at that very moment to arrest Simon and return him to Chicago in chains to face the double-murder charge.

"He [Ciolino] convinced me that he was actually trying to help me by giving me a way out before the police got to my house to arrest me. He said that if I gave a statement saying I did the crimes in self-defense that he would get me a free lawyer, that the professor would make it so I would only have to serve a short time in prison, and that when I got out, I'd be taken care of financially and would not have to work again," Simon alleged.

If Simon agreed and confessed, Ciolino promised Simon that a Chicago lawyer, a veteran member of the defense bar by the name of Jack Rimland, would take Simon's case. And Rimland would take it free of charge. All the defendant had to do was plead guilty, but—and it was a major-league "but"—he had to extend a personal apology to Green's mother and to Porter. That was key: Simon had to extend the apology for the deal to go through.

Ciolino said that Protess, a respected professor who wielded immense clout back in Chicago, would see to it that if Simon pleaded guilty and extended the apologies, the resulting prison sentence would be short, no more than a two-year stretch. It was an iron-clad guarantee, and here is why it all made sense to Simon—when Simon finished doing his time, just twenty-four months, Ciolino assured him, there would be millions of dollars waiting for him on the outside. Again, book deals and Hollywood movies that would generate so much money Simon would never have to work another day in his life.

Simon again erupted in anger, again professing his innocence, again declaring the whole thing was crazy. At that point, Simon alleged Ciolino "put his hand on his gun and said that we could do this the easy way, or we could do it the hard way, but either way, I was going to give a statement." Ciolino also told Simon, according to court documents, that "people have accidents" in their homes all the time, and Simon could very well have one that morning.

Up all night, the effects of booze and cocaine tapering off, Simon caved. He signed a statement prepared by Ciolino, declaring that he had killed Hillard because Hillard was going for a weapon and Green, accidentally, because she had gotten in the way. Remarkably, at Ciolino's direction, Simon rehearsed a confession prepared earlier by Ciolino. Equally remarkably, Simon then donned a T-shirt, at Ciolino's request; took a seat in a living-room easy chair; and, after Ciolino pulled out his video equipment and rolled the tape, solemnly read the confession that had been scripted by Ciolino.

That evening, February 3, 1999, CBS Channel Two in Chicago aired the taped confession, sending members of the press and public howling with indignation mixed with disbelief.

In a July 2002 *Chicago Magazine* article, Ciolino gave the following explanation of how he was able to extract the Simon confession:

"We just bull-rushed him, and mentally he couldn't recover." According to the magazine piece, Ciolino added that he, Ciolino, had "danced to the edge in getting Simon to confess," acknowledging that the "witness" in the Ciolino tape actually was an employee of the detective's.

The following day, Alstory Simon, sitting in the backseat of his sister's car, was driven to Chicago where, accompanied by his attorney Jack Rimland, he surrendered to police and to Tom Gainer, a Cook County assistant state's attorney, at the station house at 51st Street and Wentworth Avenue. Following an appearance before a judge, he was ordered locked up, where he would remain until sentencing, which was six months away.

At about the same time Simon confessed, Rita Carlisle, Inez's sister, stated in an affidavit that she and Inez were chauffeured to the offices of Martin Abrams. Ciolino shared an office with Abrams and arranged for him to represent Inez in getting her obstruction of justice charge dismissed. Rita asserts in an October 8, 2003, affidavit that four important aspects about the Abrams meeting were clear:

1. Inez, with whom Rita was very close, never once mentioned the shootings.
2. Inez lied about the shootings because of the huge payoff she thought she was going to get from Protess.
3. Abrams, who heard Rita had claimed on a Milwaukee TV station that she believed Alstory was innocent, told her that "she should keep her mouth shut" about future proclamations of Simon's innocence.
4. Finally, Rita claimed that Abrams told Inez that if she did not stick to her story—as laid out in her affidavit and averred on TV—she would be breaking the law and would go to jail.

I   February 22, 1999, Cook County grand jury testimony of Shawn Armbrust.
II   January 15, 2003, civil deposition of Paul Ciolino.
III   February 22 1999, Cook County grand jury testimony of Shawn Armbrust.
IV   January 15, 2003, civil deposition of Paul Ciolino.

6

Anthony Porter
Goes Free

The years 1998 and 1999 were not salutary for Cook County State's Attorney Richard Devine.

Prompted in part by apparent prosecutorial bungling of recent high-profile criminal cases, some involving the death penalty, the *Chicago Tribune* on Sunday, January 10, 1999, launched a five-part series titled "Trial and Error: How Prosecutors Sacrifice Justice to Win." Leaning heavily on innuendo, the award-winning series by reporters Maurice Possley and Ken Armstrong purported to document hundreds of examples of prosecutorial misconduct in Cook County and around the country and expose how prosecutors' illegal and unethical practices had been "tacitly encouraged by job promotions for some of the worst offenders."

The series pulled no punches and was particularly critical of prosecutors in Illinois. On January 11, the second installment, subtitled "The Flip Side of a Fair Trial," led with a raw, seemingly implausible anecdote. This was the tale of a newly hired assistant state's attorney on his first day on the job, puzzling over the presence of a bathroom scale on the floor outside a judge's chambers. After asking a veteran prosecutor why the scale was there, he was told that it was for the "Two-Ton contest." Inquiring further about the Two-Ton contest, the new assistant was informed that there was an ongoing competition among prosecutors to be the first to convict defendants whose combined weight totaled 4,000 pounds, or two tons. Men and women, upon conviction, were taken into the hall and weighed, the veteran prosecutor explained, and since most defendants were black, the competition was also labeled "Niggers by the Pound."

The opening piece on Sunday, bearing the subheading, "The Verdict: Dishonor," gave the impression that prosecutors not just in Cook County or in Illinois but across the country were either stone incompetents or villains of the darkest spirit. From Illinois to Texas, Louisiana, and other states, prosecutors seemingly routinely concealed "evidence suggesting innocence or presented evidence they knew to be false," the article stated. And Land of Lincoln prosecutors ranked near the top of the list for such wrongdoing.

"Illinois's record for misconduct by prosecutors is particularly abysmal," the Sunday installment found. "Of the 381 people whose homicide convictions were reversed, forty-six were tried in Illinois. That's the second-highest total and twice as many as the state that ranks third. Only New York State, which is more populous," had a bleaker record.

The *Tribune* was not alone in its attack on State's Attorney Devine and his assistants. The Medill Innocence Project and its probe of the Porter conviction not only would not go away, it was gaining a full head of steam as the team gathered first Taylor's recantation, and then Jackson's, and media outlets all over Chicago, most prominently WBBM-TV, carried stories on the recantations, taking indirect shots at Devine's office in the process.

What's more, at the time of the *Tribune* series, Devine, the Cook County Board, and attorneys for the freed Ford Heights Four men were knee-deep in talks to reach a financial settlement over claims that the four had been wrongfully prosecuted. Two months later, those talks would result in a board-approved taxpayer payout to the defendants and their lawyers of $36 million.

The previous November, as was noted earlier, Northwestern Law School held its first annual three-day National Conference on Wrongful Convictions and the Death Penalty to much public acclaim. High on the agenda of the conference had been a discussion of the "systemic flaws" in the U.S. criminal justice system in Illinois and elsewhere.

Warden, cofounder of the first annual conference, made his position well-known among attendees. "In Illinois capital cases, and I am confident that the error rate probably holds true across the country, [the error rate] is approximately ten percent. That means that for every ten people that we have executed, it is very likely that one of those people was innocent," he asserted. "The scary thing about it is that the guilty or innocent issue is just the threshold when it comes to capital cases. It is still being applied in an arbitrary, capricious, wanton, freakish and racially discriminatory manner."

The external noise triggered backbiting, finger-pointing, division power struggles, and general all-around recriminations and disorder within Devine's office, even at the highest levels. Any large state's attorney's office is by nature intensely politically attuned, and a highly public controversy is certain to set in motion a cascade of less-than-noble machinations. Nearly a thousand prosecutors toiling at the Criminal Court Building at 26th Street and California Avenue and at a dozen or so city and suburban branch courts were suddenly beginning to be depicted as bumbling fools, if not scoundrels.

Dick Devine was a cum laude Bachelor of Arts graduate of Loyola University in 1966 and a 1968 cum laude graduate of Northwestern University School of Law who had served as managing editor of the *Law Review*. In 1999 he was in the third year of his first four-year term as Cook County's chief law-enforcement officer. His intent was to seek a second term in the upcoming November 2000 election cycle, and the boiling-hot, internecine bickering was not helping his reelection plans, particularly as snippets of the infighting routinely appeared in the press. And it could not have been helping Devine's emotional well-being.

When the blockbuster news broke on WBBM-TV Channel Two and was picked up by other news outlets, that Alstory Simon had let fly with an out-of-the-blue February 3 confession to Porter's crimes and that the confession was videotaped, and that Simon's estranged wife had supported that claim, also in a video and an affidavit three days before, the raging turmoil inside Devine's office flew off the charts. Morale among Devine's ranks collapsed.

"Double Murder Case Unravels," wailed a February 4, 1999, front-page *Chicago Tribune* story, a blowup photo of exuberant students LaBorgne, Rhodes-Pitts, Rubinsky, and McCann just below the masthead. "Once two days away from execution, inmate may go free." Black-and-white head shots of a glum-looking Alstory Simon and a beaming Anthony Porter accompanied the story, which was picked up by newspapers and the electronic media across the country.

"Evidence Grows That Wrong Man Is on Death Row," announced a column by the *Tribune's* Eric Zorn, who at times seemed a virtual publicist for the Medill Innocence project, though an unpaid publicist. The column began: "Inez Simon always knew that, one day, the knock would come on her door and the haunting past would rush in. Last week it came. Two female journalism students from Northwestern who had tracked her through a network of her relatives and other tips appeared at her home in Milwaukee with cryptic news."

Amid blistering criticism that an innocent man had spent seventeen years behind bars and at one time was only fifty hours away from being executed, Cook County Criminal Court Chief Judge Thomas Fitzgerald, at the request of a beleaguered Devine, ordered Porter's provisional release from jail on February 5. The release was provisional as Porter was still, at least technically, under an Illinois Supreme Court order to undergo a mental fitness hearing, which had just begun but was continued by the judge for ninety days.

A jubilant Porter walked out of Cook County jail around 1 P.M. on February 5, sporting dreadlocks and a deeply lined face and clad in black jeans and a black jacket. He jumped into the opened arms of Professor Protess, the professor's clapping students standing nearby, broad smiles on their triumphant faces.

"It feels marvelous to be outside," said Porter. "I'm free," he declared. To Porter, the outside world "looked great," adding that he could not wait to get home and see the family. Eat a steak dinner. He went on to say that it was his "faith in God" that enabled him to get through his nightmarish ordeal.

Asked if he was bitter toward prosecutors, Porter replied, "They've got a job to do but they took too damn long to get me out of here." The former death-row resident also said he was thankful for Simon "stepping up" and taking blame for the murders.

At the time of Porter's release, First Assistant State's Attorney David Erickson noted that the charges against Porter had not been dropped, but in light of the sensational new twist in the case, releasing Porter "was the appropriate thing to do." Erickson stated that the investigation was ongoing and declined to speculate what the future held for Porter and his legal issues.

With Porter's release, the press went into overdrive. "Doubts about Death Penalty," "NU Professor Now a Media Superstar," "Porter Case Spurs Pressure for Reforms," rolled the headlines while the electronic media played repeated footage of the prisoner's release and interviews with Protess and the students.

Beneath the headline, "Convict Freed After 16 Years on Death Row," the *New York Times,* in a February 5, 1999, article put it this way:

"In an extraordinary move, prosecutors here have arranged for the release of a man who spent 16 years on death row and came within a breath of being executed for a double murder it now appears he did not commit. The inmate, Anthony Porter, wore a half-stunned, half-exultant smile as he walked out of prison today. Gone were the prison jumpsuit and the handcuffs. Gone, too, was the hard, flattened look of a man who has been condemned to die. And the first thing he did was to make a beeline for the people whose effort, it seems, has saved his life: five journalism students at Northwestern University and their professor, who investigated the case and found evidence that led another man to confess to the murders this week."

Even Tom McCann got into the act with a story he wrote for the *Daily Herald,* ten days after Porter was freed. In his February 14 "Special to the Daily Herald," bearing the headline, "How We Got Porter off Death Row," McCann wrote, in part: "I began this case believing what I read on paper. I was a sheltered suburbanite from Park Ridge who had never even driven through the slums of the South Side. I'd never gotten a speeding ticket, much less a confession beaten out of me. I had no idea of the helplessness poor blacks face when they run up against a legal system ready to lock them away. I was mildly pro-death penalty until we uncovered the real story behind the stacks of papers."

The freeing of Porter was raising eyebrows in the Illinois governor's mansion in Springfield as well. In fact, the following year, January 31, 2000, then-Illinois Governor George Ryan would declare a moratorium on executions of any more Illinois death-row inmates—the first time any state had taken such action. The governor said the moratorium would remain in place until a blue ribbon commission, appointed by him, conducted a review of its past implementation and issued a report on it. He cited the Anthony Porter case as a reason for the moratorium.

"I now favor a moratorium, because I have grave concerns about our state's shameful record of convicting innocent people and putting them on death row," Governor Ryan said in announcing his historic action. "And, I believe, many Illinois residents now feel that same deep reservation. I cannot support a system, which, in its administration, has proven to be so fraught with error and has come so close to the ultimate nightmare, the state's taking of innocent life. Thirteen people have been found to have been wrongfully convicted." Ryan was noting that that since the death penalty was reinstated in Illinois in 1977, twelve death row inmates had been executed while thirteen had been exonerated. "How do you prevent another Anthony Porter—another innocent man or woman from paying the ultimate penalty for a crime he or she did not commit?" the governor asked, rhetorically.

There is no doubt that the turmoil in the Cook County State's Attorney office was being viewed with some concern by the "Man on Five"—that would be Mayor Richard M. Daley sitting in his fifth-floor office at City Hall. Mayor Daley, who was running for re-election to a fourth term in the upcoming February 23 election, had been Cook County state's attorney when the Porter arrest, trial, and conviction took place. His first assistant at the time was Richard Devine, who occupied that position from 1980 to 1983.

Daley's mayoral opponent, U.S. Representative Bobby Rush, was hammering away at what he called Daley's cavalier attitude toward the overturned Ford Heights Four convictions and the Porter case, which had been prosecuted while Daley was state's attorney. No doubt re-election would be a layup for Daley. Still, it was no time for bothersome election distractions, particularly among members of Illinois's Black Caucus.

Out of this media maelstrom and in the wake of Porter's release there emerged a fateful decision, not by Devine, but by one of his top assistants, a man named Thomas Epach. Epach had completed his undergraduate schooling at Valparaiso University and was admitted to the Illinois bar in 1979 following graduation from Loyola Law School. He was Chief of the Criminal Division under Devine in 1999. Epach was deeply troubled by his boss's hurried decision to release Porter without conducting a hearing of any kind. A hearing, for example, to revisit the evidence against Porter during his 1983 trial or to investigate the merits of the videotaped confessions of Alstory and his estranged wife, Inez, and the affidavits of Taylor and Jackson.

Without Devine's knowledge, Epach ordered a promising young assistant state's attorney by the name of Thomas Gainer, who would go on to become an Associate Cook County Criminal Court judge, to impanel a grand jury in February and determine two things: Who pulled the trigger that killed Marilyn Green and Jerry Hillard in the Washington Park pool grandstand in 1982; and what were the methods and merits of the Medill team investigation that in less than one hundred days had upended a conviction that had been affirmed time and again by state and federal judges in Chicago all through the 1980s.

7

The February 1999 Grand Jury

Cook County Assistant State's Attorney Thomas Gainer, a 1977 graduate of The John Marshall Law School, took seriously his marching orders from Epach. By the tone and scope of his inquiry, it's clear that he went into the grand jury having done his homework on all facets of the Porter case. He was a sharp prosecutor who consistently and persistently asked insightful questions. Although the grand jury was an "informational" proceeding, as opposed to a criminal proceeding, Gainer called eleven witnesses and carefully questioned almost every one of them. Oddly, though, given his understanding of other facets of the case, the exception was Ciolino, whom he never asked about Simon's forced confession.

The first set of witnesses were five individuals who seventeen years earlier had been in the Washington Park pool and had observed different aspects of the fatal shootings of Green and Hillard. They were four friends, Kenneth Edwards, Eugene Beckwith, Michael Woodfork, and Mark Senior, and a fifth individual, Edward Taylor, who also was in the pool with his buddy Kenneth Williams (deceased in 1999) at the time of the shootings. The second set of witnesses consisted of members of the Medill team—Protess, Ciolino, and Protess's four students: Syandene Rhodes-Pitts, Shawn Armbrust, Tom McCann, and Cara Rubinsky.

The proceedings bear the Cook County designation GJ#363. In the end they accomplished two things. First, when Gainer finished questioning the five pool witnesses, he had in effect reconvicted Porter of the 1982 murders and exculpated Simon. Second, when he finished with the six members of the Medill team, he had demonstrated that the Medill investigation was at best unprofessional, and at worst an almost-total abrogation of any concept of journalism, its operation under the aegis of one of the nation's top journalism schools notwithstanding.

The grand jury hearing begins with the testimony of the 1982 pool witnesses, leading off with Kenneth Edwards, who with the late Henry Williams was one of the State's two most important witnesses at Porter's 1983 trial. After Edwards was sworn in by Gainer before the grand jury on February 17, 1999, Gainer first told jurors that this hearing was "a 'John Doe' investigation relating to the deaths of Jerry Hillard and Marilyn Green." He added, "We are not seeking an indictment at this time."

Under questioning by Gainer, Edwards, thirty-eight at the time of his appearance, told grand jurors that he had lived in the Washington Park area all his life, that as a youngster growing up he considered the sprawling park as his "backyard," and that he had known Porter and members of his family all his young life. At the end of the Bud Billiken Day Parade on August 14, 1982, he said he and two friends, Eugene Beckwith and Michael Woodfork, were in the park playing softball when they met up with another mutual friend, Mark Senior. Subsequently, he testified, the four of them decided to buy some beer and sneak into the closed Washington Park pool and go for a swim, as it was a warm and muggy evening.

Edwards testified that he and his friends had entered the pool sometime after midnight by scaling the fence at the north end and were walking along the edge of the Olympic-sized pool when Edwards said he spotted Tony (Anthony) Porter seated at the top row of the bleachers at the north end alongside three other individuals.

He said that he and Beckwith stripped down to their trunks and were horsing around on one of the smaller pool's two diving boards when he heard the sound of gunfire and looked in the direction of the shots—the top row of the bleachers at the north end, right where he had spotted Porter when he entered the pool. He said one of the shooting victims was stretched out on the bleacher while a second victim, a woman, had risen up and was staggering down the stairs. As for the assailants—for Edwards said there was more than one person, who has never been identified—they were walking calmly down the bleacher stairs.

GAINER: As you sit here today, can you tell this grand jury who it was who fired those shots?

EDWARDS: I sure can.

GAINER: Who was it?

EDWARDS: It was Tony Porter.

GAINER: And the people that you saw coming down the stairs calmly before the woman started to stagger, do you know who either of those two people were?

EDWARDS: One was Tony Porter. The other guy I did not know.

Toward the end of the session, a juror asked Edwards another question.

JUROR: Now that you have seen pictures of Alstory Simon in the newspaper, could that other person have been Alstory Simon?

EDWARDS: No, it could not have been.

JUROR: Why would Simon say he did it now and he didn't say it then?

EDWARDS: Your guess is as good as mine. It just makes me laugh that the situation [is] the way it is now.

William Taylor, another pool witness, gave a sixteen-page

sworn statement on February 10 to grand jurors. Taylor began by acknowledging that he and Henry Williams, his now-deceased friend, also had entered the north end of the locked pool between midnight and 12:30 A.M. on August 15, 1982 by scaling the pool fence.

Taylor testified that he stripped down to his swimming trunks, leaving his clothes in a pile next to a wall where Williams was seated; jumped into the pool; and swam four laps, "focusing on my swimming technique and breathing control." After several minutes, Taylor said he climbed out of the pool and began putting his clothes back on when he heard a noise, as in the sound of gunfire, and looked to the upper bleachers at the north end where the gunfire had come from.

TAYLOR: I saw a man running down the bleachers past me. I saw a gun in his hand.

GAINER: Now, the person that you saw running down the bleachers, as you sit here today, who was that person?

TAYLOR: It looked like Anthony Porter.

GAINER: And that person that ran down the bleachers, you say he ran past you?

TAYLOR: Yes, he did.

GAINER: Do you know as you sit here today who that person was?

TAYLOR: It looked like Anthony Porter.

Beckwith, who testified on February 9, rendered a narrative not dissimilar to that of Taylor and Edwards. He and the three others scaled the fence at the north end of the closed pool, and as they were headed for a dip in the Olympic pool, Beckwith told his listeners he spotted four persons seated at the north end at the top of the bleachers, one of whom he recognized as Anthony Porter. As with Edwards, Beckwith was not able to identify the fourth person in the group.

He said he jumped into the pool, swam a lap or two, exited the water, and climbed a diving board where he was jumping up and down and hollering to his friends. It was then that he happened to look to the north end of the bleachers when one of the four persons "stood up and shot two of the other ones." He said the two assailants walked away from the killing scene, while one victim lay prone across the bleachers and the other, a woman, stood up and staggered down the stairs.

JUROR: Were you able to recognize any of the two people that walked away from this, from the shooting?

BECKWITH: One of them was Tony Porter.

Mark Senior testified that he too scaled the fence at the north end, spotted four people seated in the top row of the bleachers, and identified one of them as Anthony Porter. He too heard sounds of gunfire, but because he was at the far south end of the pool, he said he was unable to identify the gunman. As for Woodfork, he also heard the sound of gunfire come from the north end of the upper bleachers but likewise was unable to identify the assailant because he, like many others in the bleachers that evening, fled from the pool for fear of getting shot.

Asked if Senior and his friends knew Anthony Porter, the witness replied, "Everyone knew him...by name. I don't think they ever associated with him. We tried not to associate ourselves with— at that time what we called the bad guys of the neighborhood."

As is often the case with eyewitnesses, particularly of a violent crime, the testimony is not precise; the key is that despite the turmoil, all witnesses put Porter in the park, when he says he was not. All saw him standing next to the victims before the gunfire. And all saw him leave the scene.

The sworn testimony elicited by Gainer from the Medill team— Protess, Ciolino, and Protess's four students—makes it painfully clear that the Medill probe was next to meaningless, and had its efforts been examined even cursorily by the media or the office of the state's attorney, Porter never would have been freed and Simon never incarcerated. Included here are some of the highlights of the four Medill students' testimony, each of whom appeared before the grand jury on February 22.

The transcript of the testimony of Tom McCann, who had become a de facto leader of the team, runs in excess of sixty pages. McCann began by saying he enrolled in Protess's News Media and Capital Punishment class in the fall of 1998 and that he opted to investigate the Porter case out of the four cases that his professor had presented to the class. The purpose of the course McCann described as "a class on how the media can play a role in death-penalty cases to, you know, see if there was a wrong committed or if everything is fine...a watchdog role."

After describing for grand jurors how he and Ciolino obtained the Taylor affidavit in November 1999, McCann made a startling admission, especially for one who said he was taking a course that teaches one how to play a media watchdog role in death-penalty cases. He admitted that he was aware of four other witnesses, all friends—Kenneth Edwards, Michael Woodfork, Mark Senior, and Eugene Beckwith—who were in the pool and had told police in 1982 that they witnessed one aspect or another of the Porter shootings as that episode unfolded. Yet McCann acknowledged that he never interviewed those witnesses.

GAINER: Did you do anything to investigate them?

McCANN: No.

GAINER: Did you go out and talk to them?

McCANN: (in a convoluted response) When I was doing this, it was only Anthony Porter...and when we got William Taylor's affidavit, we didn't look back at the other ones.

GAINER: But, Tom, what did you tell us your purpose was, what were you doing this for?

McCANN: To find the truth. But I am a college student. I mean this took a long time. I mean this took a long time.

GAINER: Let's go with that. You are a college student, I understand that. Who told you to quit when you got to the Taylor affidavit?

McCANN: No one. We only had a very short time so we decided to look at the alternate suspect.

GAINER: Did anyone tell you to go back and see whether or not they saw Porter in the stands that night?

McCANN: No.

GAINER: Did you think for a minute that might be important?

McCANN: I did not.

Gainer returns to the issue of why the Medill team didn't interview the four friends who had witnessed various aspects of the double homicide.

GAINER: Did anyone tell you not to interview those four guys?

McCANN: No.

McCann continued, sounding almost as though he were complaining, in a somewhat confusing explanation. "This is a class. And, you know, we didn't have much time. I mean go to the places where you will find the most information. You know it is either to the places where you will find the most information. You know, it is either to these people or go to the people that were actually there. So we decided not to waste time because, you know, we had three other classes to go to and just try to talk to the people that we thought were close to it."

Syandene Rhodes-Pitts, a native of Houston, a senior at Northwestern majoring in Broadcast Journalism, and newly enrolled in Protess's winter-quarter Investigative Journalism class, also made her appearance before the Cook County grand jury that February day. Rhodes-Pitts began by telling her listeners that she had spent the 1998 fall quarter, from September 28 through mid-

December, earning college credits while working as an intern reporter for a Topeka, Kansas, television station.

On January 4, 1999, the first day of the winter investigative
journalism class, she testified that she chose to join the student
team that was continuing the investigation of the Porter case. The
other members of the class who chose to do the same were returning veterans McCann, Armbrust, and Rubinsky. Erica LaBorgne,
the fifth member of the team, like Rhodes-Pitts, was a newcomer to the group and had no inkling what the case was all about.

Rhodes-Pitt said that before the first day of class she had never
met the other team members, had never discussed the Porter case
with anyone, and had no clue who Porter was. Her testimony cen-
tered largely on a second trip—in mid-January—that she, attorney Sanders, McCann, and LaBorgne made to Division Nine of
Cook County Jail to visit once again with a shackled Porter.

She testified that during the jail visit she asked no meaningful
questions of Porter and that because of her reticence, and that of
her companions, she had gained little new or significant information about his case—his trial, his alibi, his guilt, his appeals,
his previous episodes of violence. Nothing.

When Gainer asked Rhodes-Pitts whether she had spoken with
Porter during her first and only visit with the prisoner, she told
the grand jury that she said, "Hi. I am Syan Rhodes. I am one of
the people on the team."

"Do you remember what he said in response?" Gainer asked.

"He said hi."

What is stunning about Rhodes-Pitts's grand jury appearance
is not her uninformative answers to Gainer's questions. Rather, it
is how she responded to a series of questions put to her by a grand
juror after Gainer was finished. Beginning on page 46 of Rhodes-
Pitts' grand jury transcript, one of the grand jurors weighs in, and
when that juror is finished with the witness, Protess's overriding

goal—the objective of setting Porter free and incarcerating Simon—is clear.

JUROR: Hearing your story, hearing the professor's story, hearing other witnesses' stories gives me the impression that it's entirely possible at times that you might be a pawn.

RHODES-PITTS: Who might be?

JUROR: You.

RHODES-PITTS: Me, myself?

JUROR: You, and other students, possibly a pawn, and so we are trying to find out. It's not a...you know, we need to know the facts. All we can know. If there is...is there any television connection to all of this, is there a big story, a book, is there...what is motivating the move toward this direction where there is a lot of evidence that you have admitted that you have seen but passed over blindly perhaps without giving it a second look, it's not being investigated and...

RHODES-PITTS: I don't think I understand.

JUROR: I am sure you don't, because you don't know...you've been asked and you've indicated that you don't know, and yet you should.

RHODES-PITTS: Are you saying is there a movie motivating what, like television...

JUROR: Could be anything. An innocent man being railroaded. A guilty man being let loose. It makes a great story.

RHODES-PITTS: What are you saying?

JUROR: I am saying it's a lot of money.

RHODES-PITTS: And your question is?

JUROR: I am saying that you are a part of it and don't know anything about it.

RHODES-PITTS: I know what I've been doing for the past month and that has been investigating Anthony Porter's innocence.

JUROR: Or guilt. He might be guilty?

RHODES-PITTS: The class I am taking is investigative journalism and we were given the case because there was no evidence linking him to the crime.

JUROR: What would you say is your objective of the assignment you were given?

RHODES-PITTS: I believe the objective would be to find any evidence, interview anyone you could that would lead you to freeing this man.

JUROR: Your objective is freeing him not just investigating all of the facts?

RHODES-PITTS: Right, investigating the facts, and as the facts... as we had read the facts, there was no physical crime, physical evidence linking him to the crime, therefore, we proceeded with innocence.

JUROR: I guess what I am suggesting is we have different stories about the objective of your class course, whether it's about investigative journalism, whether it's about trying to get someone who has in a court of law been found guilty to be...

RHODES-PITTS: I am sure you have been provided with a syllabus which would probably outline Professor Protess verbatim, but as far as where I was coming from, that's what I gave you, you know, that was my objective.

The February 22, 1999, testimony of Shawn Armbrust, the student at whose parents' Brookfield Wisconsin house Ciolino videotaped Inez Jackson's confession, follows a similar path. Armbrust began by telling grand jurors the purpose of the new Protess class, the News Media and Capital Punishment.

"The course description contained, I think, you work on real-life cases of miscarriages of justice or potential miscarriages of justice and also participate in the National Conference on Wrongful Convictions and the Death Penalty."

On September 28, the first day of the class, which met from 3

P.M. to 6 P.M. on Mondays, she testified, she, McCann, D'Angelo, and Rubinsky were treated to an hour-long lecture by Protess, followed by a two-hour panel discussion among Protess; Rob Warden, at the time a coauthor with Protess of *Promise of Justice* about the Ford Heights Four case; and two of the Ford Heights Four, Dennis Williams and Kenny Adams. She said the three-hour session had been arranged at the behest of Ken Bode, Medill dean at the time, and that the program drew 250 university students and professors.

During the month of October, she said, much of the team's time was spent meeting with Dan Sanders, Porter's attorney, and wading through his files; Appolon Beaudouin, the investigator with the Appellate Defender's Office in Chicago, who led them to affidavits incriminating Simon in the pool murders; and Larry Marshall, the professor at Northwestern's Law School who was working on a strategy to save Porter's life. Paul Ciolino, the private eye who was part of the team, also was present.

Three aspects of Armbrust's testimony are noteworthy. One is her December 16 jail visit to meet Porter with Protess, Sanders, McCann, and Rubinsky in attendance. The second is why she believed Porter was innocent. And the third is an extended exchange she had with a grand juror who was deeply troubled about the fact that she and Rubinsky met alone with Simon in his Milwaukee home.

Regarding the December 16 jail visit, Gainer asked the witness if she had asked Porter any questions and if so, what sort of questions were asked.

ARMBRUST: I think I just asked him how he was doing. I mean, they were pretty basic questions...I asked him how his headaches were because he gets very bad headaches...I learned that from his lawyer.

And, by December 16, when she and the class were convinced

more than ever that Simon was the real pool killer, she acknowledged under questioning that she knew little about Porter's case, including his alibi that he was in a Taylor Homes play lot at the time of the murders.

GAINER: Did he tell you whether or not he was in the park that night?

ARMBRUST: He told us that he was not in the park that night.

GAINER: Did you investigate this alibi pursuant to your assessment of the case?

ARMBRUST: No.

GAINER: As you sit here today, do you know anything about his alibi?

ARMBRUST: I know that his alibi was that he was at his family's house.

GAINER: And how did you learn that?

ARMBRUST: I think from my professor.

GAINER: Did you ever read the transcript of the testimony of his alibi witnesses that testified at his trial?

ARMBRUST: No.

The questioning on this subject resumed a little later in Armbrust's testimony.

GAINER: Is that the total of all of your conversations that you had either personally or overheard on that occasion concerning his alibi?

ARMBRUST: Yes.

At the tail end of her testimony, a grand juror engaged Armbrust in a tight exchange about her trip to Milwaukee with Rubinsky and Protess.

JUROR: It surprises me that you and your girlfriend Cara would be up there talking to Simon, and the professor, as smart as he is, is in the car. Why didn't he have some protection for you going up to see Simon if he had any thought that he might be the killer?

ARMBRUST: First of all it was our interview. Second of all, we are...we weren't confronting him that he committed a crime. We were just interviewing him and...

JUROR: Two young white girls?

ARMBRUST: Quite frankly he would be pretty stupid to do anything to us. He knew our professor was in the car. He knew what we were there about. He...he would be pretty stupid to have done anything to us.

JUROR: You're naïve to do something like that. If you were my daughter, I'd—

ARMBRUST: My parents knew I was there.

At that point, Gainer jumped in. "Your parents were aware that you were in this guy's house when your professor believed that he had committed a double murder?"

ARMBRUST: Yes.

Gainer also asked her why she and her fellow students did not interview Beckwith, Senior, Edwards, and Woodfork.

ARMBRUST: We didn't because they said...they all said it was too dark to see anything anyway. I think that's what I thought they said.

At that point, another grand juror asked Armbrust what it was about the jail meeting that made her so certain Porter was innocent.

She answered, "Well, the reason we were going to meet with him was to ask him if he had committed the crime, but the first thing he said was that he was innocent, and I heard people say that before, but he was more convincing."

Following the jail visit, Armburst said she raced over to McClurg Court, home of WBBM-TV Channel Two, to be present when Taylor read his affidavit to the station's evening viewing audience.

Finally, there is the student testimony of Cara Rubinsky of Pittsburgh. In her forty-one pages of testimony, she begins by acknowledging that she had not read Porter's alibi witness testimony, the fingerprint report, or the pathologist's report and that she, like her fellow students, took no notes during the jail encounter. Thus, her recollection of events was foggy.

At one point a grand juror asked her why the visitors "didn't have an audiotape or cassette of any kind." Rubinsky replied, "It was just a meeting to get to know him, so we didn't really feel like it was necessary."

However, she was able to give the clearest picture of the encounter she and Armbrust had during their December 9, twenty-minute interview with Simon, while their professor remained in his car across the street.

"Alstory told us that...he said he hadn't been in the park that night, but that he and his wife [Inez] had been with Marilyn and Jerry. He told us that they were all walking toward the park and a group of men who...he said the name about a gang, but I am not sure if they were a rival gang, but he said there's a group of men on the other side of the street. He thought it was like trouble and that he warned Jerry and Marilyn not to go into the park."

She continued, "He told us...I think he said that he and his wife went for ice cream and brought it back, the kids were at home, and they brought the ice cream back to the kids at home."

She too testified about a mid-January visit she made with Shawn Armbrust and Dan Sanders to Cook County Jail to visit with Porter. Again, she said no one took notes, Dan did most of the talking, and she did not ask Porter a single question about his case.

"I didn't speak with him much. Mainly I was listening to his conversation with Dan. I just mostly said, 'Hello. How are you doing?' ...I just spoke with him just, 'How you doing? Hello.' That was it."

Asked whether she had read the police reports that contained interviews with Edwards, Woodfork, Senior, and Beckwith, she said that she had.

GAINER: Did you make any attempt to interview any one of those four people?

RUBINSKY: No.

GAINER: Did anyone suggest to you that you do so?

RUBINSKY: We talked about doing it but hadn't gotten around to it by the time other stuff came up.

Professor Protess also made an appearance on February 22, 1999. He began by providing jurors with a brief sketch of his professional background. He was a contributing editor and staff writer at the *Chicago Lawyer* for five years, when the monthly was owned by Warden; a research director at the Better Government Association between 1976 and 1981; and a political science professor at Loyola University from 1973 to 1976. He said he obtained a Ph.D. from the University of Chicago in Public Policy, and by the time of his grand jury appearance, he had been teaching at Medill for eighteen years.

According to his testimony he, like the students, had only sparse knowledge of the Porter case. He told jurors that while he had read Taylor's testimony at Porter's 1983 trial, he had not read the alibi testimony put forth by "Fat Luke," that he had not read the testimony of Henry Williams, nor had he read any of the police reports on the four other witnesses who had put Porter at the pool the night of the shootings.

As he had with the others, Gainer took the professor to the December 16 jail visit with Porter. Protess said the shackled prisoner repeatedly attested his innocence during a five-minute outburst. "I am innocent, I need you to believe me. I have been saying this for sixteen years. I'm innocent," Protess quoted the prisoner as saying.

In sync with other earlier grand jury testimony, Protess said the prisoner believed that Alstory Simon and Inez Jackson were the villains and that Walter Jackson, incarcerated in Danville, would be able to prove Simon shot Hillard and Green. And also in agreement with earlier testimony, the professor acknowledged that Ciolino had obtained two Chicago lawyers for Inez and Simon after their videotaped confessions in Milwaukee—attorney Jack Rimland for Simon, attorney Martin Abrams for Inez. This led Gainer to probe further.

GAINER: Did anyone ever say to you, you should look at whether or not your investigator is paying for the lawyers of Simon and Inez?

PROTESS: No...my assumption was that the two lawyers were doing this on a pro bono basis.

Critically, Gainer then got the witness to acknowledge one of the strangest shortcomings of the 1999 journalism class. Like the rest of the Medill team, Protess admitted that he was fully aware that there were four witnesses—Edwards, Woodfork, Senior, and Beckwith—who identified Porter as the killer. Protess first acknowledged that the testimony of Woodfork, Edwards, Senior, and Beckwith accords more with Porter's guilt than Simon's, after which the following exchange took place.

GAINER: And your students didn't investigate those four men, did they?

PROTESS: No.

GAINER: You didn't ask Paul Ciolino to find those four men?

PROTESS: No.

GAINER: You didn't go out yourself and look for those four men?

PROTESS: No.

GAINER: None of your group ever [tried to] interview any of those four men?

PROTESS: That is correct.

Gainer also inquires of Protess about the December jail visit with Porter. And the professor is no more interested than his students in exploring the defendant's alibi or any other critical elements relevant to the case.

GAINER: Do you recall any other things he said?

PROTESS: It was. Yeah. "I am innocent. I need you to believe in me. I have been saying this for sixteen years. I'm innocent." He just said it over and over again. "You guys have got to believe me." And then from there the conversation went into questions that I had about who he thought might have been responsible for the crime if he was innocent.

GAINER: What did he say when you asked him those questions?

PROTESS: He said that he thought Alstory Simon and Inez Jackson were responsible.

Later, Gainer asked the witness how the jail meeting ended. Protess said Porter "concluded the conversation by expressing his gratitude for our willingness to investigate his claim of innocence and then he hugged all of us."

The next important witness was Paul Ciolino, who was forty-two at the time he appeared before the grand jury on February 17. Unlike his questioning of the students, Gainer's focus seems less determined with Ciolino. For example, the prosecutor never explores how it is that an Illinois-licensed private investigator with a checkered background, is associated with one of the nation's leading journalism schools and is working pro bono for Medill.

He never delves into questions about how Ciolino appeared uninvited at Simon's front door, and how, after Simon allowed him and a fellow investigator in, Ciolino obtained a double-homicide confession from Simon who is alone and without an attorney.

The prosecutor asked no questions about how Ciolino got two Chicago criminal defense attorneys, with close ties to Ciolino, to represent Simon and Inez for free.

Nor did Gainer ask any questions about who paid their fees, though it turned out to be Ciolino who fronted the monies.

Strikingly, Gainer listened without interruption as Ciolino engaged in a lengthy narrative as to how he ultimately forced a confession from Simon. Ciolino began by relating how he told Simon that Chicago news outlets, including Eric Zorn of the *Chicago Tribune,* have been reporting all week about how he is now believed to be the true Washington Park killer and how he then aired a videotape for Simon in which a black actor, hired and scripted by Ciolino, claimed to have witnessed Alstory shoot the two victims, ultimately forcing Simon's confession.

Ciolino testified that initially Simon claimed his innocence until Ciolino and his sidekick, Arnold Reed, showed him the signed affidavits of Joyce Haywood, Ricky Young, and others who claimed Simon was the killer. Wonder of all wonders, Ciolino went on to describe how Simon's TV, which just happened to be turned on and tuned to Channel 50, a CBS affiliate in Milwaukee, was airing at that very moment the video of Inez claiming she was with Alstory the night of August 14–15, 1982, and that she saw him fatally shoot the couple.

"And me and Alstory walked over to the TV and there was the whole story, about three-and-a-half minutes of why Alstory Simon committed this murder on network news. And Alstory is sitting there watching it and he's staring at it and he's listening to the whole thing. So everything that I just told him about, the media, he's seeing it for himself.... And I had no idea this was on.... It just happened."

When the news segment ended, Ciolino testified that he turned to Simon and said, "A man has been sitting in prison for seventeen years for a crime you committed, and isn't it time you stood up and act like a man and take responsibility? And Alstory looked at me and he says, 'I shot them two people, but I didn't mean to do it.'"

8

The $2 Stickup and the Sentencing of Alstory Simon

Following the videotaped confessions by Inez Jackson and Alstory Simon the Porter case moved rapidly. On February 2, 1999, Gainer filed an emergency motion for Porter's release. Judge Fitzgerald ordered that release on February 5.

But also at Gainer's request, the release was to be provisional only. In his emergency motion, Gainer also asked that the Porter fitness hearing, which actually had begun the week before, be suspended until a complete investigation could be undertaken in light of the compelling new evidence developed by Protess and his students.

Fitzgerald granted the request and delayed the fitness hearing for ninety days. At the time, First Assistant State's Attorney David Erickson told members of the media that the charges against Porter had not been dropped, but in light of the sensational new twists in the case, releasing Porter "was the appropriate thing to do." Erickson also said that the investigation was ongoing and declined to speculate as to what the future held for Porter and his legal issues.

In early March, Gainer issued a report based on his grand jury questioning of the pool witnesses and the Medill team. The Gainer report concluded, in part, "We must not now blindly cling to those jury verdicts of guilty of murder, as solemn as they are, given all that has come to light in this unique case."

Based on Gainer's findings, Judge Fitzgerald on March 11 vacated the murder and weapons charges against Porter. In so doing, he told a packed courtroom that he was "profoundly grateful that we have spared the unthinkable conclusion to this case." Oddly, however, kept in place was the armed robbery charge against Porter that stemmed from the two dollars Porter took from Williams at the end of a loaded pistol on August 15, 1982.

That development led to a line of reasoning that was tough to reconcile with Porter's seeming exoneration. If that charge was valid, then why was Porter being released at all?

State witnesses said Porter was in the park, and he shot the couple after robbing Williams of two dollars at gunpoint. At trial, Porter's alibi witness Fat Luke testified that Porter never was there at all. But now, the murder and weapon charges have been dropped, yet the armed robbery offense has not been removed, meaning that Gainer believes Porter was in the pool area and that he robbed Williams. What is more, Porter was in the pool area and robbed Williams only a minute or so before the victims were killed. Finally, the evidence shows that Porter robbed Williams only a few yards from where Hillard and Green were shot dead. Despite all of this, Gainer is saying Porter should be released and the weapons charges dropped, a point of view that seems to contradict the remaining charge.

When asked why the armed robbery was not tossed out along with the murder and weapons charges, Gainer said, "We believe that the evidence, at the time and now, is sufficient to prove him guilty beyond a reasonable doubt."

The decision not to scrap the armed robbery charge triggered protests from the media. With that charge still in place, Porter would go to trial—or plead guilty—and if he was convicted, his lawyers would have a difficult time winning sympathy for their client and winning a larger jury award at the wrongful conviction civil trial that was certain to come.

"Retrial for $2 Holdup May Cost Him Millions," a September 14 *Tribune* headline blared, the story noting the same thing: with an armed robbery conviction, it would be all the more difficult to win a huge award from a civil jury.

"Unless some important justice issue would be served putting Anthony Porter on trial a second time for a robbery he allegedly committed 17 years ago, the state's attorney's office should end the case," the *Chicago Sun-Times* wrote in an editorial, failing to explain how he could have pulled off the armed robbery when he was in a Robert Taylor Homes playground.

This is really one of the more bizarre twists of logic in this case. Either Porter was in the pool area or he wasn't. Either he had a weapon, and used it to rob Williams, or he did not. Arguing that it was unjust to subject Porter to a retrial for the armed robbery on the grounds that he was already unfairly prosecuted for murder makes no sense at all.

Porter's attorney Sanders was clearly aware of this. After the hearing, Sanders noted that he intended to ask that the remaining armed robbery charge be dropped as well. And a couple of months later that charge also was vacated by Fitzgerald, removing a final impediment for a completely vindicated and ultimately pardoned Porter to sue the City of Chicago and others for millions of dollars.

The following September 7, media attention throughout Chicago was again fixed on the courtroom of Judge Fitzgerald when a court bailiff pounded the gavel and shouted out, "People of Illinois versus Alstory Simon." The defendant, a giant of a man who had been locked up in Cook County Jail since shortly after his confession and arrest in Milwaukee, lumbered into the courtroom under the watchful eyes of armed sheriff's deputy police.

Simon had agreed to plead guilty to the Washington Park shootings, and he was about to be sentenced to some heavy time. Simon's situation was what is called a "heater case." His confession had been aired time and again throughout the Midwest—and occasionally nationwide—by the electronic media, and rehashed, parsed, and editorialized about by newspapers. A drumbeat of sorts had set in among reporters, fueled in the main by Protess's nonstop feed of Porter exclusives to WBBM-TV Channel Two News and other media outlets. Following the initial blockbuster airing of Inez Jackson's video and Simon's sensational confession, the rest of the media had rushed to grab a piece of the story.

Taking the story at face value and without expending any effort to examine the background of the headline events, editorial pages and columnists had been understandably indignant. The very idea that Porter had spent all those years on death row, that he was only fifty hours from being put to death before the Illinois Supreme Court intervened and granted a stay in late 1988 was a must-include line in virtually all news accounts.

As Simon stood before Judge Fitzgerald, awaiting sentencing, there was not a single reporter in the courtroom who had read the original 1,200-page Porter trial transcript. Not one knew a thing about the evidence that led to Anthony Porter's original conviction. None knew a thing about Porter's playground alibi. None knew that a CPD officer named Liace had stopped and frisked Porter as Porter hurried from the scene immediately after the murders. None had an inkling that Porter had shot Earl Lewis in the head after Lewis objected to Porter kicking his dog. None knew a thing about McGhee's pool-bleachers thumping. Perhaps most importantly, not one was aware of the outrageous circumstances surrounding Simon's confession.

If Simon had any supporters, they might have convinced themselves not to worry. All these facts would be made known to Judge Fitzgerald during the sentencing hearing. That was the purpose of the hearing, after all, to see what cards each side was holding, had Simon declined to confess and the case proceeded to trial. Only seven months before Assistant State's Attorney Gainer had reprised the entire Porter/Simon debacle during his grand jury probe of Protess, his students, and the Medill School's unusual relationship with Paul Ciolino. Gainer had heard the testimony of eyewitnesses Eugene Beckwith, Mark Senior, Michael Woodfork, and Kenneth Edwards, testimony that had exculpated Simon and inculpated Porter. Fitzgerald would hear about it.

And if Gainer faltered, just wait until Jack Rimland, a prominent member of the defense bar, got his licks in. Rimland was no one to trifle with. A graduate of DePaul University College of Law, the attorney had thirty-five years of experience in criminal defense in the state and federal courts, and he had worked on numerous death-penalty cases in the past. Had Simon been ready to mount a defense, he had every reason to expect his competent, experienced attorney to present all of the exculpating facts during his hearing.

Late on February 4, after his client had been arrested in Milwaukee, Rimland told *Tribune* reporters, "Obviously, if he [Simon] is charged, he's looking at the death penalty." That, of course, was an unusual thing for a defense attorney to say, publicly stating that one's client was facing execution before he had his day in court. But, an informed observer might have hoped, Rimland would set the record straight, clean up that indiscretion. His client was innocent until proven guilty.

The wholesale deprivation of his client's rights by the gun-toting Ciolino and cohort Arnold Reed would be brought to light. Threats against his client's life would be revealed. The house of mirrors that had been fabricated that day by Ciolino and Reed. The videotape of the unidentified black man—later identified as an actor hired and scripted by Ciolino—accusing Simon of the shooting deaths. The spotting by Ciolino of the CBS news report in the wall mirror. The whole sordid, unethical extraction of a "bull-rushed" confession.

Rimland would bring it all out, lay the skullduggery bare for Judge Fitzgerald, who after hearing it and seeing it would call a halt to the proceedings, order an inquiry—a reset back to day one.

Judge Fitzgerald opened the hearing by underscoring its purpose and its solemnity, telling Simon, "There are certain things I have to tell you, what this conference contemplates. That I will be told about the plea agreement that apparently has been reached by your attorney and the state's attorney. In addition, I will be informed of the facts of the case, the evidence that they expect to produce during the trial of the case." The judge went on, explaining how the hearing would unfold, what additional facts would be disclosed, who would say what to whom, and then, looking down from the bench, Fitzgerald asked the defendant, "Do you want me to proceed?"

"Yes," Simon replied.

Despite Fitzgerald's assurances, the facts underlying the case never were brought to the court's attention, either by Gainer or Rimland. This omission has never been explained.

Gainer went first. He opened by telling the judge that present at the proceedings were Offie Lee Green, the mother of Marilyn Green, and Katrice Green and Earl Green, Marilyn's two children, who were five months old and four years old, respectively, when their mother was gunned down.

Then the prosecutor moved directly to the guts of the State's case against Simon.

"Sometime shortly after midnight this defendant with a woman by the name of Inez Jackson, his girlfriend at the time, and the two shooting victims, Marilyn Green and Jerry Hillard, all four of them were seated in the bleachers at the Washington Park pool.

"Now, it was the day or the early morning hours after the Bud Billiken Parade.... Hillard and Green, the shooting victims, were friends of Simon and Inez Jackson. The four of them were in the park sharing some alcoholic beverages and conversation...."

The prosecutor then asserted that if Inez Simon had been called as a witness at trial, she would have testified that Hillard sold drugs for Simon, that Simon became aware that Hillard was withholding drug sales proceeds from Simon, and that an argument erupted. Inez would testify, the prosecutor went on, that she heard a gunshot, that she saw Hillard fall back onto the bleacher steps, and that she turned in the direction of Green and heard more gunshots.

Had she been called as a witness, Gainer informed the judge, Inez also would have testified that she departed the park in Simon's "grasp," that the two, on the lam, lived first with Inez's uncle, then in an apartment in the Chicago Housing Authority's Stateway Gardens at 3500 S. State Street, then in an apartment on the West Side, and finally in Milwaukee, where they have lived ever since.

The State also would bring out Simon's three previous robbery convictions, the most recent dating to the early 1980s. The prosecutor also said the State would call witnesses Mark Senior, Michael Woodfork, Kenneth Edwards, and Eugene Beckwith. But Gainer uttered not a word about their exculpatory testimony—exculpatory testimony that Gainer long ago had known about and had heard again with his own ears as recently as the previous winter, during the grand jury proceedings he conducted. And nothing was mentioned regarding the testimony of the late Williams and Taylor, which led to Porter's 1983 conviction. Nothing. Not a word.

Before Judge Fitzgerald a travesty unfolded. Gainer droned on about forensic experts, about a police officer by the name of Billy Johnson whose testimony was irrelevant to Porter's or Simon's case, about the Bud Billiken Day parade, about causes of death determined by the medical examiner's office, bullet entries, bullet exits, detritus found at the murder scene.

Gainer also told Judge Fitzgerald that had this case gone to trial the State would have called a witness by the name of Paul Ciolino. This was an utter outrage, knowing, as Gainer did, the bizarre and illegal ploys the private eye with the checkered past engaged in to extract the illegal confession from Simon.

Rimland was even worse, at least from the perspective of anyone who hoped Simon would be vigorously represented. The lawyer's failure to disclose material facts to his client or the sentencing judge defies explanation.

Rimland never conducted a presentence investigation of his own. He did not interview the witnesses against Porter—Woodfork, Edwards, Beckwith, and Senior—who had signed statements identifying Porter as the killer. He did not investigate the genesis of the black man on the video, nor did Rimland tell his client that the putative eyewitness was in fact an actor hired by Ciolino and told by Ciolino what to say on the video.

Rimland failed to tell his client that he could file a motion to suppress evidence, based on the confession coerced by Ciolino. He didn't tell Simon that he, Rimland, was being paid by Ciolino. He did not disclose that at the time of the sentencing that he shared office space with Ciolino. Also occupying that office suite was attorney Martin Abrams, who represented Inez Jackson, again thanks to Ciolino who got him the referral. Nor did the judge hear about these potential conflicts of interest.

Rimland did not tell Simon that he had worked closely with Ciolino on the Simon case prior to the sentencing. He did not tell Simon that he was aware that Ciolino had coerced witnesses to implicate Simon in the murders in exchange for money and reduced sentences. In fact, Rimland allowed Simon to believe that all of the witnesses had implicated him even though, like Gainer, he knew that several witnesses implicated Porter and made no mention of Simon at all.

Rimland filed no motion challenging the alleged confession. He never requested a fitness hearing for his client when Rimland knew, or should have known, that Simon was "a mentally and emotionally impaired person due to his drug addiction."

Instead, he advised his client that the State had such a strong case that Simon needed to make a plea deal to avoid the death penalty. He told his client that only one witness saw Porter pull the trigger, that the witness was William Taylor, and Taylor had recanted that testimony.

One of the several bizarre segments of the change of plea and sentencing hearing took place near the beginning. In order to keep Simon bound to the game plan, Rimland told his client that if he did not plead guilty, he was facing ninety years in prison for the murder of Felix Alphonso Bello, a Cuban drug dealer who was shot dead in Milwaukee in 1983. Because of this misrepresentation, Simon believed he was a suspect in that murder as well, which he was not.

Rimland advised the court that Mark Williams, an assistant state's attorney from Milwaukee who headed up homicide prosecutions and had firsthand knowledge of the Bello murder, was present. He asked Fitzgerald if Williams could address the chief judge. After Fitzgerald agreed and asked Williams to come forward, Williams gave a brief statement suggesting that Simon had nothing to do with the Bello murder.

"Judge, we feel that the Wisconsin case against Mr. Simon is not strong," Williams said, explaining only the Milwaukee view of Simon's non-participation in a Milwaukee killing. "Further, Judge, that another reason why we are allowing Mr. Simon to do this [plead guilty] is the fact that it is clear from everyone's story that Mr. Simon did not fire any shots in the homicide. Also he was not present" at the crime scene. Williams surely must have departed Fitzgerald's courtroom at 26th Street and California Avenue that day wondering why in the world he had been asked to be present at the hearing. Why Rimland brought him to the court remains a mystery. But almost everything about Rimland's "representation" of Simon is hard to fathom.

Incredibly, four months earlier Rimland had presented awards to Protess, Ciolino, McCann, Armbrust, and three other students for their actions in freeing Porter and developing evidence against his own client, Simon.[1]

And finally, Rimland did not disclose the conversation he had had with the Reverend Robert Braun, a longtime social activist whose main mission was to shut down drug dealers in Milwaukee's inner city. Reverend Braun had forged a close bond with Simon shortly after he, Inez, and her children arrived in Milwaukee in the early 1980s. Simon had volunteered to assist the reverend in padlocking abandoned buildings where dope dealers operated and then reporting their operations to Milwaukee police. The reverend asserts later in a 2005 affidavit that when he objected to Rimland about Simon's pleading guilty to a murder he did not commit and also that Rimland had a profound conflict of interest because of his association with Ciolino and Protess, Rimland cast his response in a strange light.

In his affidavit, Braun says, "Alstory [Simon] told me that

Northwestern professor David Protess and private investigator Paul Ciolino offered him money, a movie, and a book deal, if Alstory would plead guilty. Alstory told me even though he was innocent, that Ciolino convinced him that they have enough evidence to convict him.

"I had many phone conversations with Mr. Rimland and advised him that I thought it wrong to plead Alstory guilty for a crime he did not commit. Mr. Rimland told me it was Alstory's decision alone to plead guilty."

Braun's affidavit continues, "I advised Alstory that they were using him and not to believe them because what he was doing was not right. Alstory told me his attorney, Jack Rimland, advised him to take the deal and plead guilty.

"Mr. Rimland told me that at one time he worked for both Northwestern University and Anthony Porter. He told me that there was no conflict of interest at this time because he now represents Alstory Simon."

Reverend Braun closes with this: "Mr. Rimland advised me not to attend Alstory's trial because I could cause problems, and he did not want anything to change Alstory's guilty plea."

There was one more thing Rimland had advised was "a must" at the hearing. If the promised two-year prison sentence and subsequent book deals were to go through, Alstory had to extend a personal apology to Marilyn Green's mother, Offie Green, and the victim's two children, all three of whom would be in court. The apology was required, Rimland told Simon.

Before the hearing ended, Gainer told the judge that Offie Green would like to approach the bench and say a couple of words. After Judge Fitzgerald allowed the move, Offie rose from her chair, approached the defendant, looked Alstory Simon directly in the eye, and said, "You came to my house that Friday, shook my hand as my daughter's friend with Inez. I would like to know, she had a baby girl five months old and son four years old, I would like to know why would you take my daughter's life and she had two kids and you shook my hand as my friend.... What did my daughter ever do to you?"

As a blanket of silence fell across the jammed courtroom, Alstory Simon, in a move that, taken alone, is as tough to comprehend as Rimland's or Gainer's questionable conduct, extended a lengthy apology to Offie and to Porter. "First of all, I would like to apologize to Miss Green. I know it won't bring her daughter back. I'd like to apologize to her grandchildren. I never meant to hurt Miss Green. This was, started off as a friendship, turned into a tragedy that I have had to live with for the last seventeen years. And I never meant to harm or hurt anyone actually.

"I am sorry that Anthony Porter had to suffer for seventeen years on death row. I never knew that anyone had even been arrested or accused of a crime. Because I had moved out of the State of Illinois.

"I was never the type of person to really watch television. Because I was too busy wrapped up trying to maintain a life for myself, trying to do the right things. Trying to stay out of trouble.

"And all I could say is, is that I am sorry, Miss Green, and the little ones, that this ever happened. And that I hope that they can find it within themselves to forgive, which I doubt. It would be very hard to... She was a wonderful person...."

Simon's apology solidified his guilt in the minds of those in the courtroom who had no deep knowledge of the case. Even an observer who knew all of the facts surrounding the 1982 murders would find it baffling.

Before imposing sentence, Judge Fitzgerald made a few remarks that in retrospect could not have been wider of the mark. As the packed gallery listened in silence, the judge offered a short but lofty soliloquy.

"The law is always an effort to reach a balance between the parties between issues, to try to do that which is right. I think the plea agreement in this case is one of those efforts.

"I think that we all ought to remember that the business we are in deals, both sides of the case, so dramatically with human lives that we ought to approach each and every case as if it is the only case and the most important case.

"Hopefully, this case can remind us that that is what our business is. We ought to be compassionate to those who have suffered loss. We ought to be just to those who are charged with crimes."

With that, Judge Fitzgerald sentenced Simon to fifteen years in prison for the charge of voluntary manslaughter for the death of Marilyn Green, a sentence he ordered to run concurrently with the thirty-seven-year prison term he imposed on Simon for the murder of Hillard.

---

1   Rimland was president-elect of the Illinois Attorneys for Criminal Justice, and on May 7, four months before Rimland stood before Fitzgerald on behalf of Simon, he presided at an organization dinner. At the gathering, Rimland presented awards to Protess, Ciolino, McCann, Armbrust, and three other students for their actions in freeing Porter and developing evidence against his client Simon. In presenting the organization's annual Advocacy Awards, Rimland said: "David Protess and his students utilized their talents as investigative journalists and successfully uncovered crucial evidence resulting in the freeing of Anthony Porter. Our organization honors them for the extraordinary effort they demonstrated in establishing Porter's innocence before his execution date."

9

The Long Road to Freedom

When Alstory Simon's confession to the pool murders was aired by WBBM-TV Channel Two at 6 P.M. on February 3, 1999, Jimmy Delorto was sitting in his desk chair in a cluttered, unpretentious basement office in a western Chicago suburb watching the newscast on an ancient, oversized TV on the other side of the room. He removed the cigar he had been puffing on, turned to his partner, Johnny Mazzola, whose attention also was glued to the set, exhaled, and in unison with Mazzola said, "What a crock of shit."

The February 3 newscast also featured short takes reviewing the work of Protess and Ciolino and the relentless effort of the four students in reversing the seeming injustice that had been visited on the once doomed-to-die Anthony Porter.

"Here we go again," Delorto added.

Delorto grew up in Chicago's Little Italy, near Taylor Street and Racine Avenue, and Mazzola was a native of Chicago's Southwest-Side Gage Park neighborhood. They are retired Federal Bureau of Alcohol, Tobacco, and Firearms agents who for more than forty-five years combined had worked some of Chicago's most unforgettable crimes. Notable among them were the 1977 disappearance of the sixty-five-year-old candy heiress Helen Brach and the abduction and murders of the Schuessler/Peterson boys, a triple homicide that shook Northwest-Side Chicago residents to their cores in 1955. Their resumes also included numerous undercover probes of organized crime.

Following their retirements from the government on the same day in 1995, the two nearly lifelong friends became private detectives licensed by the State of Illinois, and they hung a Delorto Mazzola & Associates shingle outside their office in the basement of a wood-frame house they own in Batavia, a town on the Fox River, west of Chicago. What caused the pair's instantly jaundiced reactions as they listened to the Channel Two report of Alstory Simon's confession was the fact that the two sleuths also had worked the Ford Heights Four case: Delorto and Mazzola had encountered the work of Professor Protess before and had come to know something about the Medill journalism professor's modus operandi.

The Ford Heights Four had been exonerated and freed in the summer of 1999, with a huge assist from the three female Protess students. Almost immediately Freeborn & Peters LLP, a respected mid-sized Chicago law firm had been hired by Cook County to prepare for what was inescapably coming next: a massive damages lawsuit by the four men for their wrongful arrests, convictions, and incarcerations. Freeborn & Peters, in turn, hired Delorto and Mazzola to assist in putting together a blow-by-blow chronology of the protracted, twisted history of the case as the law firm prepared to defend the County and perhaps several sheriff's police investigators who had handled the investigation.

A brief sketch of this legal saga is in order.

In 1978 William Rainge, Kenneth Adams, Dennis Williams, and Verneal Jimerson were charged with abducting Lawrence Lionberg and his fiancée, Carol Schmal, early in the morning on May 11, 1978, from a Clark gas station in Homewood where Lionberg worked and where Schmal had dropped by for a visit. The captives were driven to Ford Heights (then known as East Chicago Heights), a poor municipality near the Indiana border with a largely African-American population. The couple was marched to an abandoned townhome at 1528 Cannon Lane, where the defendants allegedly took turns raping Schmal while Lionberg was held captive in the basement. Schmal and Lionberg were then murdered.

Early on May 11, Lionberg's body was discovered by a couple of youngsters looking for a can to play kick-the-can. The young man, lying face-down in a gravelly, weed-filled area, next to a creek behind the Cannon Lane townhome, was wearing a brown leather-type jacket and a pair of partially bleached blue jeans. A subsequent autopsy by Dr. Robert J. Stein, Cook County's Chief Medical Examiner, concluded that Lionberg died of three bullet wounds, two to the back of the head, a third in the center of his back.

Schmal's body was found by an East Chicago Heights fireman about thirty minutes later. She was on the second floor of the abandoned townhome, lying on her stomach in a prone position on top of a pair of pink jeans, naked from the waist down with the exception of a pair of knee-high stockings. Her other clothing, a pinkish, light-colored sweater, was pulled up, and a white bra was draped over her shoulder. Dr. Stein, who initially reported "semen and fecal matter adjacent to her buttocks," also concluded that she had been shot twice in the back of the head at close range, about six to twelve inches away.

The same .38-caliber pistol, which never was recovered, had been used to kill both victims.

The arrests of Rainge, Adams, and Williams (and later Jimerson, hence the Ford Heights Four) followed two early breaks in the case.

The first break was a tip to Cook County Sheriff's police from Charles McCraney, a would-be blues artist and a resident of East

Chicago Heights. He told police he had been practicing his guitar in the early hours of May 11 when he heard a commotion outside his home. He said he looked through his second-story window and saw Williams, Rainge, and Adams, all of whom he recognized from the neighborhood, enter the Cannon Lane townhouse with three or four others. About thirty minutes later he said he heard the muffled sound of gunfire "come from the direction of 1528 Cannon Lane. Owing to the echo, he believed that the shot had been fired indoors," according to a report prepared by the Cook County State's Attorney's office following the convictions of the Ford Heights Four.

The second break involved Paula Gray, also an East Chicago Heights resident. Gray, who suffered from mild cognitive disability, lived with her mother and her twin sister two houses from the murder scene. At 7:30 P.M. on May 13, she traveled to the Sheriff's Police substation, which was then in Homewood, with her mother and her twin sister. There she gave a detailed account to police investigator Patrick J. Pastirick of the horrific ordeal she witnessed inside and outside the abandoned townhouse at 1528 Cannon Lane early that morning.

She repeated her testimony a short time later the same evening to Cook County Assistant State's Attorney Ernest DiBenedetto, who, assigned to the Night Felony Review Section, had arrived at the Sherriff's Police station to assess the unfolding investigation. Paula gave the same testimony a third time five days later, on May 16, during an appearance before a Cook County grand jury.

Her account begins with Paula telling Pastirick that at about 11 A.M. on the morning of May 11, she told her twin sister, Paulette, and her mother, Louise Gray, that there was a white girl lying dead on the upstairs floor of the Cannon Lane townhouse. She told the investigator that her mother and sister demanded she report it to authorities at once. Her mother had reminded her that she had always cautioned her daughters to tell the truth because the truth can never hurt.

A summary of a portion of her testimony, as outlined in court documents, follows.

She first asserted that defendant Williams pointed to the house and told the white couple to walk on the back street of Cannon Lane and go into the vacant townhome at 1528 Cannon Lane. Upon entry to the abandoned townhouse, the lady was taken upstairs. "The lady went first, then Dennis and then me, and Kenny and then Verneal (aka 'Lurch') and Rainge (aka 'Tuna') was downstairs with the man."

Once upstairs the defendant Williams gave Paula a lighter and told her to light it so that he could see what he was doing. He then laid the woman down on the floor, took her boots off, her pants, her panties, and he put the boots in the closet. Defendant Williams then unzipped his pants and he lay on top of her and she looked at him. The woman said, "Please don't hurt me."

Defendant Williams had sexual intercourse with the woman, got up, pulled his pants up, and then Lurch, Verneal Jimerson, pulled his pants down and got on top of the woman. Lurch stayed on top of her having sexual intercourse for half an hour and then he got up and pulled his pants up. Then defendant Adams unzipped his pants, pulled his pants down. He got on top of her and then she looked at him and he didn't stay down there too long.

Defendant Williams then told Lurch to go downstairs. Lurch went downstairs and Tuna, defendant Rainge, came up and Tuna unzipped his pants and pulled his pants down and he got on top of her. When Tuna got up, defendant got back down and had sex with her again. After defendant Williams got up, Tuna unzipped his pants, got back down and had sex with her again. When defendant Rainge got up, defendant Williams told Adams to "come here." Paula said, "Please don't do it again," and Kenny said, "Okay I won't." So he stayed over there by Paula. When defendant Adams declined his second turn, defendant Rainge went downstairs, and Jimerson came upstairs, unzipped his pants and lay on top of the woman again.

When Jimerson was finished, defendant Williams turned her over onto her face, reached into his front pocket and took out a black gun. Defendant Williams pointed the gun and shot the woman twice in her head.

Defendant Williams then took Paula's hand and they all went downstairs to where the man was being held. He knew what had happened and he was "shaking all over." They took the man outside and over to the creek where they "flipped him over the hill." The man was lying with his face down on the ground and defendant Williams shot him twice in the head. Defendant Rainge then shot the man once in the back.

Defendants Williams and Rainge and Paula then "walked over by the creek and Dennis throwed (sic) the gun in the creek where I showed the police and then we walked back." Defendant Williams told her not to "tell the police; if I do, he is going to come back and kill me and my family and then he got in the car and took Lurch home."

There was a third critical State witness: David Jackson. On the morning of May 15, 1978, he was being held in the lockup at the Markham Police Station where he saw the defendants Williams, Rainge, Adams, and Jimerson, people he recognized from the neighborhood. Later the five men were taken to the "bullpen," a holding cell at Cook County Jail. There, Jackson later would testify, he heard the four discussing the May 11 murders in graphic terms.

One exchange Jackson later would testify to: "The defendant Dennis Williams spoke to Tuna saying he 'had a shot of pussy the night before,' with Tuna responding, 'Yeah man, I had something the night before too. I didn't really need none.' Jackson said they all agreed they 'really shouldn't have took (sic) it from the lady.'"

Again, according to Jackson's testimony, "Defendants Williams and Rainge said that they were 'glad' that they 'took care' of the guy, 'popped him in the head,' because 'he just kept running off at the mouth.'"

After Gray's testimony and that of McCraney and Jackson, prosecutors secured indictments against the four men.

At a subsequent preliminary hearing, however, Paula Gray recanted her testimony, saying it was "all a lie." It is worth noting that just prior to her recantation, Paula, her mother Louise, and the rest of the Gray family moved in with the family of defendant Dennis Williams, notwithstanding the fact that Williams had told Paula he would kill her and her family if she told the police what had happened.

As a consequence of the Gray recantation, charges against Jimerson were dropped, but prosecutors then indicted Paula Gray for being an accomplice to the murder and for perjury. Following a 1978 jury trial, in which the four were convicted, Williams was sentenced to death, Rainge to life, Adams to seventy-five years, and Gray to fifty years.

When Williams and Rainge won new trials in 1982, because of a conflict by one of their attorneys, Gray made a deal with prosecutors in which she now agreed to testify against Williams, Rainge, and Jimerson in exchange for her release from prison. Jimerson was charged, convicted, and sentenced to death in 1985. Two years later, Williams and Rainge were convicted a second time. The same sentences they had received the first time were imposed—death for Williams, life for Rainge. The Illinois Court of Appeals upheld Adams's sentence of seventy-five years in prison for his role in the crime.

So, at the point at which the three Medill students—Stacy Delo, Stephanie Goldstein, and Laura Sullivan—had obtained the 1996 statement from Paula Gray, setting the wheels in motion that ultimately led to the freedom of the Ford Heights Four, the woman had changed her testimony four times. During the 1978 grand jury, she gave the detailed account of the roles of each of the four defendants in the rape and murders; a short time later in 1978 and at her trial she recanted that testimony; and in the 1982 retrials of Williams and Rainge and at the 1985 trial of Jimerson she testified for the State, changing her testimony a third time.

The fourth revision of her testimony came during her tearful interview with the three Medill students in 1996, saying she had lied to investigators in 1978 because they told her if she didn't implicate the four defendants, she would spend the rest of her life in jail. In addition, she said that investigators had kept her in a hotel room for three days, cutting her off from her family and community and subjecting her to nearly nonstop interrogation.

But it wasn't just the erratic testimony of Paula Gray in the Ford Heights Four case that led Delorto and Mazzola to refer to the 1999 televised broadcast of Alstory Simon's confession to the Washington Park pool murders as "a crock of shit." It was another Protess involvement in the Ford Heights Four case that, among other things, struck them as far beyond the pale of journalism standards.

While working on the report for Freeborn & Peters, Delorto and Mazzola came across three documents—two crafted by Protess and another by a St. Anne, Illinois, police officer. Taken together, the documents revealed for the first time, but not the last, that in order to ferret out "the truth," Protess would not hesitate to offer money, fame, and movie rights.

The first document is a memo written by Steve Abrassart, a St. Anne police officer, and sent to his supervisor, Sergeant Don Flett, also a St. Anne police officer, in 1996. The Abrassart memo, dated March 27, 1996, bears a 1:58 P.M. time stamp. Its subject is Dave Protess.

In the two-page memo, Abrassart reports to his boss that he had spoken to "two college-age, female white young ladies" who were standing outside St. Anne police headquarters, 122 S. Chicago Avenue, at about 6:30 P.M. on March 13, 1996. They were seeking directions to Charles McCraney's house, who by then had moved from Ford Heights to St. Anne, a dusty rural municipality of about 1,000 inhabitants located near the Indiana border just south and east of Kankakee.

Abrassart's memo goes on to say he was puzzled why "two white females wanted to go to Willow Estates," the St. Anne neighborhood in which McCraney lived, and particularly to visit with McCraney. At the time, McCraney was living with his wife and four children in a run-down, two-room wood-frame house that was without running water, was heated by a wood-burning stove in the middle of one of the two rooms, and was surrounded by two dozen or so junked cars.

After the two students explained they were working with their college professor, Protess appeared, identifying himself initially as "an investigator working on a criminal case out of Cook County." After asking for identification, Abrassart said the professor produced an Illinois driver's license and a Northwestern University faculty identification card.

Abrassart reports that he then took Protess and his students to McCraney's house in Willow Estates. Finding McCraney away from home, the trio left two notes "for Charles," one affixed to the inside of his garage door, the second "with a neighbor who had driven up looking for a car part." Abrassart reported that Protess and the two students then jumped into a 1994 forest green Infinity, four-door automobile, license plate number LYD 880, and with Protess at the wheel, they drove off.

Abrassart concludes with the observation that Protess and the students had made a bizarre offer to him before leaving. "They did ask me if I wanted my name in the book they were writing and I said no."

Then there are the two Protess documents, one the handwritten note left by Protess on the inside of McCraney's garage door on March 13, the other a typed letter, dated March 14, 1996, to McCraney.

In the scrawled note, left at McCraney's home, Protess wrote to the State's most important witness in the conviction of the Ford Heights Four:

> Charlie,
> Stopped by to see you about something important.
> Have information for you that should be helpful financially. [underscore Protess] Please call me at 708-491-2065. If I'm not in, leave your number and I'll call you back right away.
> Dave Protess

The March 14 typed letter made matters murkier. Bearing the heading, "Northwestern University, Evanston, Illinois 60206-2101, The Medill School of Journalism," the five-paragraph typed letter bears a handwritten postscript and is signed "David."

> Dear Charlie,
> It was good meeting you today.
> You do have monetary rights to your story, but only if you get past the inconsistent statements you've made in the past and simply be straight about what you actually saw on the night of May 10, 1978.
> What "inconsistent statements?" For one thing, please see the enclosed *Chicago Tribune* column: Is the truth what you first told Lt. George Nance, or what you later said to other law enforcement officials? Did you have "no clocks," "one clock" or "two clocks" on the night of the crime? (Your testimony varied at each trial.) Did you see "Dennis

Williams" enter the vacant townhouse, or "six-to-eight (unidentified) black men"? Did that occur "about 3:00 A.M." as you once testified, or about an hour after watching "Kojack" (about 2:00 A.M.), when the victims probably were still alive?

I could go on and on, but I think you get the point. I easily can write this book based on your various statements—which frankly would make you look bad—or you could be courageous by telling your real story about what happened in this case. It's that simple, and it's up to you, along with the many benefits from being upfront. (The fact is Verneal Jimerson already is free and the others soon will walk. Which side are you on, the 18-year-old version that's about to lose, *badly,* or the side that's about to prevail?) [italics Protess]

You don't have much longer to wait. I'm moving ahead with my investigation and book, and the movie is sure to follow. I'm enclosing the police files on the actual killers in this case (the cops knew about them six days after the murders, yet they used you the way they used the three men still in prison), and Paula Gray's recent affidavit. And there's much more to come as you'll see on Channel 5 later this week.

Think about it, [underscore Protess] and feel free to call me anytime at 708-491-2065 if you'd like to discuss this further.

Sincerely,

David

[Then, the postscript in longhand]

We could talk a little bit at a time, if you'd like. Sometimes, the hardest thing in life is to acknowledge old mistakes all at once.

There is yet another reason why Delorto and his partner called the televised Simon confession a "crock of shit."

The Protess badgering of the State's key witness did not end with letters and a visit. On March 15, Protess, this time accompanied by Ciolino and Rene Brown, another private eye, visited McCraney at a Kentucky Fried Chicken (KFC) restaurant in Kankakee, not far from McCraney's house. The purpose of the meeting, in Ciolino's own words, was to get McCraney to change the testimony he had given at the original trial—that is, to tell Protess's version of the truth.

The three men came to the Kentucky Fried Chicken meeting with a "game plan," a ruse that they had prepared in advance, a ruse that would get the impoverished blues guitar player and songwriter to at last cave in, run up the white flag, and really "tell the truth" about what he had seen that barbaric night in Ford Heights.

The game plan included Ciolino posing as Jerry Bruckheimer, one of Hollywood's most successful producers with $6 billion in box office receipts.

McCraney showed up about two hours late, sat down with the other three, and asked for the $100 cash Protess said McCraney would be paid for the meeting. After Ciolino peeled off five twenty dollar bills (or perhaps four twenty dollar bills, as there is some dispute in the record)—an expense for which Ciolino would be reimbursed by Northwestern University—and handed the money to McCraney, Ciolino introduced himself as Jerry Bruckheimer and started in.

"I told him we were developing a movie on the Ford Heights Four case. And I said, 'Charles, we want your story on this. We want you to tell us what happened that night, what you remember and what you seen (sic). And I want the truth. And if you tell us the truth, we may be able to buy your, you know, your story, your rights to the story.'"

The meeting was brief, about five minutes, with McCraney responding, "I got to think about it."

Asked if McCraney really thought Ciolino was the Hollywood producer, Ciolino responded, "Oh, I think he bought it, yes. I don't think he knows who Jerry Bruckheimer is. I could have said, you know, I am President Clinton. I don't think he would have knew (sic) the difference."

Before McCraney departed, Protess, Ciolino, and Brown used one more ploy to try to influence the man. Protess produced a copy of the contract he had signed with CBS in producing the 1996, two-part series on the Dowaliby case.

Ciolino, still pretending to be Jerry Bruckheimer, showed the contract to McCraney, saying, "This is not yours, but this is what a contract looks like. And you can have a contract like this as well if you tell us the truth as to what happened in this case."

There is a second official report outlining the March 14, 1996, KFC meeting with McCraney. This one is dated March 20. It is signed by Tom Pritchett and Sean McCann, investigators for the Cook County State's Attorney's office. The purpose of the report was an interview with Charles McCraney relative to the Verneal Jimerson case.

The one-page report begins by noting that on March 20 around 11 A.M. the two investigators met with McCraney and his brother, Howard, at the Cracker Barrel Restaurant at 1020 Corporate Lakes Drive, in Matteson, Illinois. At Cracker Barrel, McCraney confirmed the March 14 KFC meeting with Ciolino and the two others, but McCraney said the meeting was unplanned and that Protess was accompanied by three other people, not two.

McCraney stated that he recognized two of the individuals—David Protess and Rene Brown—from earlier encounters with the two men. But he said he did not know the other two—one of whom he described as a black male between twenty-five- and twenty-six-years-old, overweight with a big belly; the other was a "fat, white male" with black hair.

The report continues:

McCraney indicated that Protess and the fat white male did all the talking. He advised that Protess told him that the fat white male was a millionaire who was financing the book and movie that was to be made about this case. Protess offered McCraney two hundred and fifty thousand dollars with twenty percent up front for him to come on their side.

The money was to be delivered to McCraney's house by a woman in one hundred dollar bills, and if he wanted to use the woman for a couple of days he could. Protess told him this was his last chance to join the team because Chicago's Channel 5 news was going to dirty him up over the weekend.

The Pritchett/McCann report concludes with Protess advising McCraney that Dennis Williams, one of the Ford Heights Four defendants against whom McCraney had testified, "would be getting out of jail soon and would come to see him." McCraney said he left the restaurant without finishing his meal and that when he arrived home, he received a call from Protess and that "Protess was mad." Yet McCraney would not change his testimony, despite offers of cash or threats.

Years later, on December 19, 2002, Jimmy Delorto and Johnny Mazzola interviewed McCraney. At the time, the two investigators were working for attorneys James Sotos and Terry Ekl, who were representing Alstory Simon pro bono in an effort to get Simon a post-conviction hearing. The two attorneys agreed to work the case for no fee after they read the Simon file, which had been presented to them by Delorto and Mazzola. The connection with the two retired agents was simple: Ekl and Sotos frequently used them as their investigators.

Ekl and Sotos are both DuPage County attorneys whose practices did not really intersect previously. They have separate offices in Lisle and Itasca, respectively. However, their legal work has taken them well beyond the western suburbs to other parts of Illinois and deep into the Byzantine dynamics that can weave through the politics of Cook County and its surrounding communities.

A 1970 graduate from the University of Illinois, Champaign-Urbana with a degree in political pcience and a 1973 graduate of Northwestern University Law School, Ekl is a partner at Ekl, Williams & Provenzale LLC in Lisle. He is a prodigious and, by all accounts, a first-rate litigator. He spent ten years as a Cook County assistant state's attorney assigned to the trial division between 1978 and 1988 before opening up a practice in DuPage County. Ekl has tried in excess of one hundred jury trials and more than a thousand bench trials, many ranking among the highest-profile criminal cases in northern Illinois. In addition to his criminal work, he has represented a half-dozen professional athletes and several municipalities and/or employees in federal civil rights litigation in Chicago, Mt. Prospect, Cicero, Naperville, and St. Charles.

Jim Sotos's journey to the legal profession is a bit less orthodox. A native of Chicago's West Side, Sotos attended Holy Cross High School in River Grove where he played guard on the Crusaders basketball team before injuries, anemic academics, and disciplinary issues curtailed his playing time. Upon graduation from Holy Cross, he attended Aurora College for a year-and-a-half, played basketball, and flunked out.

He worked as a bank teller for a time, and in the late 1970s he traveled to Greece where he played basketball for Panellinios, a member of Greece's top professional basketball division, which was part of the Euro League. He returned home in the early 1980s, and as he puts it, "got smart." He graduated with honors from Baldwin Wallace College in Berea, Ohio, and in 1985 he graduated from The John Marshall Law School in Chicago before opening his Itasca law firm.

Beyond having represented governmental units ranging from

the City of Chicago and the City of Naperville to the City of Paris (Illinois) and McHenry County, Sotos authors a weekly column titled "In Federal Courts" for the *Chicago Daily Law Bulletin*. He is a regular member of the lecture circuit, discoursing on relevant legal considerations before such groups as the Illinois Municipal League, the Illinois Association of Chiefs of Police, and the Illinois Institute for Continuing Legal Education Association of Governmental Attorneys in Capital Litigation.

The agents' interview with McCraney on behalf of Sotos and Ekl again reprises the Protess visits, blandishments, and threats intended to get McCraney to alter his testimony about what he saw the night Schmal and Lionberg were murdered. Though duplicative of what has already been written, it is worth discussing in some detail because it significantly fleshes out the earlier discussion.

The Delorto/Mazzola report begins with McCraney telling the agents, "He was approached by Professor Protess of Northwestern University and others who claimed to be associated with the university to change his original testimony in exchange for $250,000. Professor Protess wanted McCraney to say that he had lied during his testimony because police threatened him and his family."

It continues:

Mr. McCraney said that Professor Protess, Rene Brown, Arnold Reid, Paul Ciolino and two Northwestern University coeds all tried to get him to change his testimony. Professor Protess told McCraney he would give him 20 percent in 'up front' money for his rights in a book and movie deal which would feature McCraney as the star witness in the Lionberg, Schmal murder case.

Mr. McCraney said that Rene Brown and two white female students accompanied Professor Protess on some visits to his home. On one such meeting, Professor Protess told Mr. McCraney he could have sex with either of the student coeds if he would come over to his side. Mr. McCraney told Professor Protess he is a 55-year-old married man and he must be kidding because he would never do anything like that or lie about something so important.

Toward the end of the his report, Delorto adds, "During 1996 Mr. McCraney remembers that Professor Protess told him that he had better change his story because Dennis Williams would be getting out of jail soon and would be paying him a visit.... According to McCraney, Professor Protess warned McCraney that Channel 5 (NBC) was going to expose him as a liar very soon if he did not change his story."

McCraney told the retired ATF agents that on the day of the Protess threat, or the following day, "someone shot a gun at his house and came very close to hitting one of his sleeping children. His daughter's head was missed by just a few inches."

Fearing for his life and the lives of his family, McCraney packed his bags and got out of town, relocating to Pine Bluff, Arkansas. Despite the pressure, Charles McCraney, who is a religious man, never signed on to a book or a movie deal, sticking with his eyewitness account right up until a debilitating stroke left him unable to communicate. He never changed his story.

The unanswered question remains: Who were the real killers of Schmal and Lionberg? Delorto and Mazzola believe there were two separate groups of assailants, two teams of four males who were involved in this barbaric episode. As Mazzola and Delorto interpret all of the evidence, Schmal and Lionberg were abducted by the four men who replaced the Ford Heights Four in prison: Arthur "Red" Robinson, Johnnie Rodriguez, and two brothers, Dennis and Ira Johnson. These four men looted the gas station and kidnapped Schmal and Lionberg, taking them to the infamous location in Ford Heights. There they gang-raped Schmal while holding Lionberg captive. When they finished, Delorto and Mazzola believe, they passed the victims off to Dennis Williams, William Rainge, Kenneth Adams, and Verneal Jimerson who took their turns raping Schmal before murdering her and Lionberg. According to their own theory, Delorto and Mazzola believed that Protess had worked unscrupulously to free guilty men.

So shortly after Alstory Simon was sentenced to thirty-seven years in September 1999 for a crime he did not commit, Delorto and Mazzola knew precisely what their next move would have to be. They would have to climb into their van, make the 143.18-mile, three-hour-and-three-minute drive to the Illinois Department of Corrections prison in Danville, and talk to Alstory Simon about his case.

10

Porter Files
His Civil Suit

Little more than a year after he had been freed from prison, Anthony Porter took the next public step that the City of Chicago, the Corporation Counsel's office, and the Chicago Police Department, along with the press corps, knew was coming. On March 9, 2000, Porter filed a lawsuit in Cook County Circuit Court accusing the City and certain members of the Chicago Police Department of framing him and ignoring evidence of his innocence.

The suit was filed by R. Eugene Pincham, a lawyer, human rights activist, former Cook County Circuit court judge, and a former justice of the Appellate Court of Illinois, and Dan Sanders, the struggling young attorney who had won a spectacular legal victory in getting the Illinois Supreme Court to stay Porter's execution in late 1998.

The suit—which sought punitive and actual damages—accused the police of forcing a witness to name Porter as the killer of Marilyn Green and Jerry Hillard. It alleged that police ignored information that would have led them to the real offender and would have proved that Porter was not in the pool area or even in the park at the time of the shootings.

As the suit was being filed, Pincham, Sanders, and Porter, then forty-five, held a mini-press conference outside the Cook County

Clerk's office in the Daley Center in the heart of Chicago's Loop.

"No amount of money can compensate this man for the injustice that he has gone through," said Pincham, presumably sending a less-than-subtle message to the City of Chicago that it was going to have to dig deep when the jury returned its verdict. "But this is certainly an effort to make him whole."

Porter, who at the time was without a job, allowed that he was living with his mother on the far South Side and that, due to his having been locked up for so long, he wasn't "doing so well."

No, he wasn't. On March 23, just twelve days after his murder and weapons charges had been vacated, he was charged with two counts of domestic battery, handcuffed to a dozen other prisoners, trundled off to a sheriff's bus, and taken to Cook County Jail. He was ordered held there pending his next court appearance in lieu of a $40,000 bond imposed by Judge Gregory O'Brien at the request of the State.

The Chicago media retained its intense interest in Anthony Porter and his story in all its iterations. However, that generally supportive relationship endured a significant strain on that Sunday evening in March. Porter, who was in the South Side home of one of his daughters, got into a fight with Carlia Perkins, forty-three, one of three women with whom he has had children (Porter is uncertain if he has fathered five, six, or as many as eight children). The cause of the argument was a broken armrest inside a van belonging to a friend who had been chauffeuring Porter to various events.

According to court documents, the conflict over the armrest escalated, and Porter began punching Carlia in the "face and chest." When Evelyn, Porter's twenty-six-year-old daughter, attempted to intervene, he turned his unbridled wrath on her. A court order of protection asserted that Porter "hit [Evelyn] around her body with his fists, pulled her down the porch stairs, threatened to kill her, stomped on her left leg and hit her on her back with a beer bottle."

A family member who witnessed the attack but remained anonymous in court documents said, "It was no joke. He was hitting really hard. You wouldn't think he would do that to his own blood."

"I want people to know what kind of man my papa is," said Evelyn at the time. "I have no love for him anymore. I can't forgive him. I'm going to stay out of his life."

The charges later were dropped at the insistence of Carlia (Evelyn had moved out of state), and the press seemingly let the matter drop. But the subject remained current long enough for a range of interested individuals, including Governor George Ryan, Professor David Protess, and an array of experts, to cast blame for the vicious attacks on just about everyone and everything other than Porter himself. Porter's defenders, like Protess, called the incident "heartbreaking," but they reminded the public that episodes of such violence could be traced to the "sudden adjustment" to life outside after years behind bars.

"Here's a guy that spent seventeen years in jail and nobody did anything for him but let him sit in jail," Governor Ryan asserted. "That's part of the problem." A Ryan spokesman added that the governor was studying ways that the state might provide transitional social and other assistance in extraordinary cases like Porter's. Terry Marroquin, a lawyer with the Capital Litigation Division, explained that Porter was suffering a form of dementia related to a head injury sustained in prison that could affect the ability to reason and control impulses.

During a subsequent interview with the *Chicago Tribune,* Porter described his circumstances as rather lowly. His life remained in flux as he sought formal exoneration in the courts. He continued to suffer headaches—the same kind he had described for

Armbrust when she asked how he was doing during the December 1998, Cook County Jail meeting.

And he desperately wanted to move his family from their South Side home where he said they felt unsafe. With his limited social and job-related skills, his future was not looking promising, but he was hopeful that was going to change with the filing of the lawsuit.

Just how much in monetary damages Pincham and Sanders would be asking a Cook County jury to award their client was still unknown, but the future payout was assumed to be gigantic. After all, the Ford Heights Four had settled with the County for $36 million. Whether or not Pincham was aware of it at the time, though, sharks were circling—other lawyers smelled a big-time payday, and they were looking for ways to get a bite of it. Everyone expected a slam-dunk settlement with the City—no trial, just like the Ford Heights Four.

According to the complaint, Porter had been wrongfully investigated; framed by the police; and wrongfully charged, indicted, tried, and convicted. He'd spent all those years on death row, right next to the cell occupied by the infamous murderer John Wayne Gacy, who eventually was put to death. The best years of Porter's life had gone up in smoke. It was payback time.

At the time the suit was filed, Pincham was semiretired. But he had led a remarkable life, personally and professionally. Born into poverty in rural Alabama, Pincham earned a degree in political science in 1947 from Tennessee State University in Nashville. The following year he married Alzata C. Henry, his high school sweetheart, and enrolled in Northwestern University School of Law. As a full-time student Pincham had waited tables at the Palmer House Hotel and shined shoes to help pay his tuition. He was awarded a law degree in 1951. He went on to become a fierce advocate for the oppressed, an enormously successful attorney, a circuit and appellate court judge, and an unsuccessful candidate for mayor of Chicago. He was a lifelong member of the NAACP and a member of the American Civil Liberties Union. His involvement with the Porter lawsuit made perfect sense, considering the level of injustice Pincham believed Porter had endured.

The Dan Sanders story, by Sanders's own recounting, was virtually a polar opposite of Pincham's. He had not exactly been a stellar student while attending the University of Illinois, College of Law in the early 1990s. Nonetheless, he managed to get his law degree, and after passing the Illinois bar exam in 1994, he kicked around from one job to the next—working as an assistant to a Skokie personal injury lawyer, writing licensing agreements for a computer company, and assisting with death-row appeals cases from the Illinois Appellate Defender's office.

In the spring of 1998, however, it appeared that Sanders was going to begin to enjoy a more substantial career. It was then that Sanders, through another lawyer he bumped into at a party, connected with Porter's family members. They were looking for someone to handle last-ditch legal work to save Porter, who by then had exhausted all appeals and was on the brink of execution.

Sanders took the case. After receiving $10,000 scraped together by Porter family members in partial payment for the agreed-upon $25,000 fee, he went to work. And though Sanders never was paid in full, he soldiered on. With the help of an array of anti-death-penalty advocates—lawyers like Futorian, social workers, and law professors like Marshall—he presented evidence to the Illinois Supreme Court in early 1998 that showed Porter's IQ stood at a low 51 (see chapter 3).

Overnight, the inexperienced lawyer, who had never tried a murder case, never tried a felony case alone, was catapulted into stardom. There were numerous TV interviews. Accolades poured in. George Ryan, the governor of Illinois, called with kudos.

By the time the Porter lawsuit was filed, however, those heady days were in the past. Sanders's fortunes had plummeted. He was at the brink of personal bankruptcy, in part because of his obsession with the Porter case and the tireless work he had put in on it. He had fewer than twenty clients. Calls from bill collectors had become a mainstay of his daily life. His landlord wanted him evicted from his one-bedroom apartment for nonpayment. His car dealer wanted his Honda back because payments were in arrears. Sanders was $120,000 in debt and had dropped his health insurance to cut costs. He did that despite advice from his doctor who said he needed surgery for gallstones.

But now, apparently, his ship had arrived—and just in time. How big a payday he could expect was uncertain, but in light of the customary one-third lawyer's fee in such lawsuits, the amount would not be chump change.

In May, Sander's dreams of financial salvation blew up. In a six-line communiqué from Porter that Sanders received via fax, Porter said he was firing the attorney. Porter was hiring a new team of lawyers to represent him in the lawsuit. It was a move that prompted near-apoplectic outrage from Chicago newspaper columnists, writers, and reporters who had been chronicling every ripple in the Porter battle to win freedom, redemption, and recompense. "Moral turpitude," "a stab in the back," "an ugly betrayal," the stories and columns announced.

"He earned the glory of having saved a man from death and fittingly, he stood to earn a multimillion-dollar payday representing Porter in a civil suit he and former Judge R. Eugene Pincham filed against the city based on Porter's wrongful conviction," wrote *Tribune* columnist Eric Zorn on October 12, 2000, under the headline "Injustice System Stands to Claim Porter's Ex-Lawyer."

"But he fought on, won Porter a reprieve 50 hours before he was to die by raising the issue of Porter's mental fitness and ultimately joined with a team of student reporters, investigators and other volunteers who found the real killer and sprung Porter from prison.

"The case received national attention and was one of the main reasons Gov. George Ryan declared a moratorium on executions in Illinois. Sanders was among those hailed a hero for justice. His was the kind of story that stood to inspire lawyers everywhere to give extra consideration to long-shot pleas for help from prisoners: I should get involved! Remember Dan Sanders!"

"Then it all fell apart," Zorn added. "It was an utter betrayal."

Did it ever. Henceforth, Porter communicated in the fax to Sanders, legal representation in the civil suit would be the responsibility of his two new attorneys: Johnnie L. Cochran Jr. and James D. Montgomery.

Johnnie Cochran was born in Shreveport, Louisiana, the great grandson of a slave. He moved to Southern California, earned a law degree from Loyola Marymount University School of Law, and became a successful criminal defense lawyer. He earned global fame as the principal litigator in the team of attorneys who won acquittal for O.J. Simpson when Simpson was tried for a double murder in 1995.

James Montgomery may not have been as well-known nationally as Cochran, but in Chicago and much of the Midwest he had established himself as a fiery, successful, take-no-prisoners trial lawyer who had won a number of high-profile, multimillion-dollar personal injury cases. A former City of Chicago Corporation Counsel, Montgomery was a native of Mississippi who, like Pincham, traveled northward, getting a political science degree in 1953 from the University of Illinois, followed by a law degree from the University of Illinois in 1956.

In March 2000, about the same time Porter filed his lawsuit with his then-attorneys Pincham and Sanders, Montgomery and Cochran declared that they had joined forces and had formed a new law firm. Referring to themselves as the "Dynamic Duo" who together "lead one of the most prolific personal injury firms in the country," Cochran and Montgomery said that the new legal entity—formerly James D. Montgomery & Associates Ltd.—would now be called Cochran, Cherry, Givens, Smith & Montgomery.

Shortly after Porter fired Sanders and Pincham and hired Montgomery and Cochran, Montgomery noted that Sanders and Porter "fell out completely." Money was a big issue. "It was a mess," Montgomery said, noting that Sanders, who already had been paid a significant amount of money for his legal work on behalf of Porter, was attempting to secure additional fees from the $145,-875 in restitution Porter had received from the State of Illinois Court of Claims in May 2000 for his wrongful conviction.

Porter's girlfriend, Kimberly Allen, piled on. She said Porter had begun questioning Sanders's handling of the lawsuit, adding, "It's a concern if a client feels his lawyer is no longer fully representing him—if the lawyer is starting to put himself in front of the client."

The running feud between Montgomery and Cochran and Sanders and Pincham exploded publically during a July 2000 airing of Cliff Kelly's WVON talk-radio show, which caters to a largely African-American audience in Chicago. With Montgomery in the studio and Porter in the background of the studio attempting to drown out Pincham—Pincham and Sanders had called in—the debate over how Montgomery and Cochran had hijacked the Porter case and become attorneys of record for Porter was not pretty.

Montgomery, a highly skilled and experienced professional, claimed that he was unaware that Pincham and Sanders were representing Porter at the time that he and Cochran took over. Pincham expressed shock and disbelief. He accused Montgomery of engaging in "pure greed and disrespect" by entering a case that already had the names of Pincham and Sanders on it.

Cochran, reached for comment, said that he and Montgomery had been contacted by Porter "to look at the case and wanted us to work with the other lawyers." Saying he had a lot of respect for Pincham and Sanders, Cochran indicated that Montgomery had reached out to Pincham and Sanders but had gotten no response.

"We're not in the business of taking cases off lawyers," said Cochran, adding that the other attorneys had been unresponsive to his new client. "Mr. Porter, when he got no response [from Pincham or Sanders], asked us to come in and asked us to represent him. We did not go out looking to take cases from other lawyers, especially lawyers in the community." Cochran concluded, saying, the issue is what is best for Porter, "who was wrongly convicted, days away from being executed, measured for his coffin and who had picked his last meal."

Though Sanders put up a legal fight to keep Anthony Porter from defecting to Cochran and Montgomery, his effort proved in vain. During a hearing before Cook County Circuit Court Judge Kathy Flanagan, with Porter and Sanders standing side by side, not looking at one another or engaging in conversation, the judge ruled in favor of Cochran and Montgomery and Porter.

"It may be unfair.... It may be unjust, but every client has an unfettered right" to fire his lawyer if he feels like it. "There is nothing I can see...that prevents this substitution," ruled Flanagan.

Pincham was furious that Porter jettisoned Sanders. "What is loyalty?" Pincham asked. "This man took on a case, a hopeless case with no hope of reward. He's doing it, trying to save the man's life, and he succeeds in doing that. Now you're going to turn around and slap the man that saved your life?"

11

The 2005 Porter
Civil Trial

By the time Anthony Porter's civil trial got underway on October 31, 2005, the configuration of the lawsuit, the lawyers involved in it, and a number of dramatic external events had changed, giving the litigation a vastly different though intense backdrop and prism through which to view it.

Sadly, Johnnie Cochran had died the previous March of inoperable brain cancer. James Montgomery was wrongly convinced the City would settle for millions, as had been the case in the Ford Heights Four case. The lawsuit would now be spearheaded by Montgomery; his son, James D. Montgomery, Jr.; and a law firm associate.

External to the suit, a sea change had taken place in Illinois politics. On January 10, 2003, Governor George Ryan pardoned four men on Illinois's death row who he said suffered the "manifest injustice" of allegedly having been tortured by Chicago police into giving false confessions. A day later, in a move that brought sneers from many current and former prosecutors and cheers from death-penalty opponents, the governor commuted the death sentences of the remaining 167 Illinois inmates on death row to life in prison or lesser terms of imprisonment.

Condemning the capital punishment system as fundamentally

flawed and unfair, Governor Ryan initiated the largest such emptying of death row in history. In one sweep, the Republican governor spared the lives of 163 men and 4 women who had served a collective 2,000 years for the murders of more than 250 people. It seemed sure to secure Mr. Ryan's legacy as a leading critic of state-sponsored executions even as he faced possible indictment in a corruption scandal that prevented him from seeking reelection.

"The facts that I have seen in reviewing each and every one of these cases raised questions not only about the innocence of people on death row, but about the fairness of the death penalty system as a whole," Governor Ryan said. "Our capital system is haunted by the demon of error: error in determining guilt and error in determining who among the guilty deserves to die."

Critically, the governor, whose own legal woes with a federal investigation of him were mounting by the day, said at the time—and would repeat in the future—his unprecedented move ultimately was motivated by doubts that had been raised in the Porter case.

A week after the governor's historic move, University of Illinois, College of Law professor Francis A. Boyle nominated Ryan for the 2005 Nobel Peace Prize. News accounts at the time said Boyle's nomination of Ryan was spurred by the governor's "courageous and heroic opposition to the racist death penalty in America." In this instance, however, the governor knew less about the issues underlying Porter's case than Protess and the Medill students.

Porter's case had gained such notoriety that it became something of a touchstone in Washington, D.C. Several weeks before Ryan's Nobel nomination, Senator Patrick Leahy (D-Vermont) brought up Porter's case during a Senate Judiciary Committee hearing on John Roberts's nomination to chief justice of the U.S. Supreme Court. Leahy used the case to gauge Roberts's stance on capital punishment and the criminal justice system. Porter's assumed innocence and what it revealed about capital-case justice in the United States became received wisdom for a while.

In spring of 2003 the *Chicago Tribune*'s Cornelia Grumman, who sat on the editorial board of the paper, was awarded a Pulitzer Prize for a series of editorials she had authored the year before. She received the award for "stirring and influential editorials on the death penalty in Illinois, as part of the newspaper's extensive examination of inequities in capital punishment in America." Grumman based her editorials on the newspaper staff's continuous reporting over a three-year period or more about prosecutorial bungling and sinister dealings by prosecutors in capital cases.

In December of 2003 Governor Ryan, who had been under investigation by the FBI for years, was charged along with an associate, with racketeering, mail fraud, conspiracy, and other crimes. Cynics alleged that Ryan's magnanimous death penalty actions had been motivated by an effort to win sympathy from a future juror, perhaps an African-American or an anti-death-penalty juror, when his case was sent to the jury. These jaded observers felt Ryan was trying to "poison the jury pool."

Likewise, Porter's lawsuit had undergone a metamorphosis. By the time it was ready to be heard by Cook County Circuit Judge James P. Flannery and a jury, it had broadly changed from the time it was first filed by Pincham and Sanders. The suit now named six defendants—the City of Chicago; police detectives Charles Salvatore, Dennis Gray, Geraldine Perry, and Dennis Dwyer; and police officer Anthony Liace. The four-count suit accused the police and the City of Chicago of malicious prosecution and conspiracy.

The suit was defended by Walter Jones, son of a Chicago policeman and a former assistant U.S. Attorney now in private practice. A disarmingly pleasant and engaging person with an eternal smile on his face, Jones is well-known for his tenacious courtroom cross-examination skills. When he first got the case, Jones was inclined to advise the City to settle it without going to trial.

But upon further examination of the facts underlying the case, Jones changed his mind and received a green light from the City to vigorously defend against the Montgomery lawsuit

There were three principal reasons for his change of heart. First, there was James Sotos, one of the two Alstory Simon pro bono attorneys who, by 2005, was well versed in the Simon/Porter entanglement. Sotos knew the Montgomery complaint was without merit and urged Jones and the City not to settle.

The second reason came from Charles Salvatore, a dedicated, decorated Chicago Police detective of unimpeachable integrity who headed the 1982 investigation of Porter. Salvatore knew the Porter complaint was without merit and would be defeated summarily, which would at the same time vindicate Salvatore and Gray, his partner.

The third reason to fight it was even more compelling: an explosive October 9, 2001, memorandum generated internally by the Chicago Corporation Counsel's Office that alleged that Simon, though innocent, had been railroaded for "political" reasons.

The memorandum was authored by Michael P. Monahan and addressed to his then boss, Mara S. Georges, at the time the City's Corporation Counsel, and her first assistant, Benjamin Gibson. It's an eye-opener. For the first time it asserts what led the State to allow the Simon sentencing to go forward in 1999 when prosecutors and defense attorney Rimland knew he was innocent of the pool murders.

Monahan, an aide to Mayor Richard M. Daley at City Hall, had been reassigned to the Corporation Counsel's office around year 2000 to head up a de facto team of assistant corporation counsels charged with a single mandate: review these so-called wrongful conviction lawsuits that were coming at the City in growing numbers. They were to come up with a recommendation on which suits should be settled and which the City should defend against.

Monahan and three assistant corporation counsels, Kimberly E. Brown, Liza Franklin, and Sharon Baldwin, addressed the 2001 memo, titled "Porter v. City of Chicago et al," to Georges. Copied on the memo are three other assistants—Nicholas F. Trovato, Robert W. Barber, and Jeffrey N. Given. The memo reprises all that has been written: the facts surrounding the pool shootings, attorney Ken Flaxman's failed attempt to get a new trial for Porter in the 1980s, the various affidavits, and the Gainer grand jury testimony of the pool eyewitnesses and the involvement of the Medill team. After laying out the high points of the case's history, the Monahan memo then asserts, "Armed with five witnesses and one dead eyewitness (Henry Williams)...who placed Porter at the scene, shooting the deadly fire, it seemed strange that the State's Attorney's Office did not re-prosecute the case."

Strange indeed. The Monahan memo then goes on to explain away the strangeness in releasing Porter. "A political decision was made that this case should be put to rest because it caused too much publicity against the imposition of the death penalty, caused great doubt about the validity of death penalty punishment for mentally challenged individuals and incited a significant amount of negative press concerning death row reversals. The state's attorney's office felt that some justice was served because he [Porter] served seventeen years behind bars and any conviction for the armed robbery would be considered time served."

A "political decision" was made to release Porter and send Simon away? Some justice was served because Porter already had served seventeen years behind bars? The obvious next question then, is what about Simon? Could a "political decision" be made to put his case to rest as well?

Monahan's memo does not address that issue.

In the end, the 2005 civil trial was to be a Jones versus Montgomery duel. On its face, Jones was facing an uphill battle because certain witnesses—including Taylor—who had been allied with the prosecution in the original criminal trial were now testifying for Porter.

Much of the testimony at Porter's civil trial reprises the testimony that has already been examined: testimony that was delivered during Gainer's 1999 grand jury probe and testimony that was given during Porter's 1983 trial. However, certain aspects of the 2005 lawsuit, trial testimony, and pretrial depositions taken in the case bring some new information to the overall story.

The first notable aspect of the civil trial is that after Porter's attorneys rested their case, Judge Flannery dropped Geraldine Perry, Dennis Dwyer, and police Officer Anthony Liace from the lawsuit. In agreeing with a motion by Jones, the judge ruled that the plaintiffs had failed to bring sufficient evidence against the three individuals to keep them in the courtroom.

Also worth mention is Porter's April 1, 2003, deposition testimony, one hundred pages in which he describes his upbringing and attempts to explain certain key aspects of his original criminal trial. Under questioning by Jones, Porter responded with a range of answers that are often nonsensical and laced with half-truths and sometimes are directly contradictory of critical testimony that was given during his 1983 trial. For example, he contradicts the alibi provided by Fat Luke, asserting for the first time since 1983 that he was at home at the time of the murders, not in the Taylor play lot as Fat Luke claimed. He denies his criminal lawyer's own admission at trial that Porter was a member of the Cobra Stones street gang, and he repeatedly alters and modifies his responses.

Porter began the deposition by saying he dropped out of Chicago's DuSable High School following his freshman year, that he could barely read or write, and that he had one sister and ten brothers, one of whom, Eric, had been shot dead by the police.

He said he had been raised adjacent to Chicago's Robert Taylor public housing project and his father, Willie, would drop in occasionally to spend time with his mother, Clara Mae, and the kids before vanishing again.

He said he had quite a few common-law wives by whom he had had between five and eight children, he was not certain of the exact number. At the time of the deposition in 2003, he said he was in the throes of a divorce from Linda Parks, a Chicago woman whom he had married while on death row at Menard. He said he was unemployed, and he had never filed a federal or state income tax return in his life.

When Jones asked again about Fat Luke's trial alibi that he and Porter and others had been drinking all night at the Robert Taylor Homes play lot when the murders occurred, Porter gave an additional puzzling response. Porter asserted that Fat Luke's testimony was untrue—Porter claimed that his own alibi from the 1983 trial was false.

He denied being found guilty of beating McGhee and robbing him of $800, even though he had pleaded guilty to that crime. He also denied shooting Lewis, despite having pleaded guilty to that assault.

JONES: You also recall that you were convicted of aggravated battery on August 5, 1983, and the victim of that crime was a Mr. Earl Lewis who said that on August 1, 1982, you had placed a gun to his head and fired it at him?

PORTER: I mean my attorney told me to cop out for the crime because he say (sic) if I go to trial I'm going to get more time.

It also turned out that it wasn't just the names of McGhee, Lewis, and Green and Hillard that were entered on Porter's rap sheet. Jones and his investigators had discovered that Porter also had been convicted in 1972, when the defendant was twenty-two, of robbing Lawrence Moore at 57th and State Streets. It was another crime that prosecutors had overlooked during the 1983 murder trial, probably because it was more than ten years old. Porter had received one year of probation for that offense.

One other deposition segment worth noting is the defendant's explanation of how he spent the approximately $145,000 in restitution money he received from the State of Illinois in 2000 for his wrongful conviction. After saying he gave much of the money to church congregations that had helped him out—church groups he was unable to identify—and to his mother to help buy groceries, he admitted that he had also purchased a new Ford Navigator for $50,000. By the time of the 2003 deposition, he said he had spent all the money.

Finally, it is noted that for the first time since Porter's arrest in August of 1982, the specter of police abuse in the investigation was raised against Salvatore and Gray. This was important, as nowhere in the underlying record was there any suggestion of police abuse in the investigation and arrest of Porter until Porter's 2005 civil trial.

James Montgomery, Jr., encapsulated that alleged abuse during closing arguments. "This is a case, folks, where detectives tampered with the witnesses and sent an innocent man to a sixteen-and-a-half-year ordeal in jail on death row," Montgomery began in his hour-long closing argument. "Anthony Porter was twenty-seven-years-old on August 14, 1982. He was forty-four-years old when he was released on the governor's pardon in the spring of 1999. He therefore spent more than one-third of his first forty-four years in prison."

Montgomery than moved directly to the abuse allegation. "Salvatore was there," in a room in Area One Violent Crimes headquarters, Montgomery began. "Two more officers came in and started talking real bad to him.... They called him an SOB and a liar. They told him he murdered two people.... One took a phone book and smacked him upside his head.... They threw the book upside his head again.... That is the testimony...threw the book at him again and hit him again on the side of his face.

"Then one of them put a typewriter cover over his head and started tightening it up and he was still cuffed," Montgomery said, referencing Porter's trial testimony. "While he was still cuffed to the wall, he blacked out. They left him in the room for a long time and then they were gagging him."

A final aspect of trial and deposition testimony was this: Porter's description of the conditions of his incarceration on death row in Menard Correctional Center—conditions which are horrific and rival those of imprisonment in Europe's gallows during the Dark Ages.

When questioned by Douglas Hopson, a third Porter attorney, during his pretrial deposition about conditions at Menard, Porter began by asserting that his cell was adjacent to that of serial killer John Wayne Gacy, who had a "cold stare" and could "look right through you," and had been given free rein by prison guards before he was executed. Despite Porter's protestations, Porter claimed, Gacy was allowed into the visitors' quarters next to the "candy machine" where children were present. Porter said he spent ten years in isolation in a cell with a "fish hole" for a window in an iron door, cramped quarters crawling with cockroaches and water bugs and other vermin.

Guards, who controlled the lighting, heating, and flushing of his toilet, tormented him by activating the lights while he was asleep at night, flushing his toilet only when they got around to it, and arbitrarily turning the heat up and down. They spat in his food, put cockroaches in his food, and taunted him about what he wanted for his last meal and what kind of coffin he wanted until "it just broke me down and I'm still hurting now."

Finally, there is the October 9, 2002, deposition of William

Taylor, who found himself, yet again, being questioned about the pool murders, this time in preparation for Porter's 2005 civil trial. He had discussed that testimony many times before, including with McCann and Ciolino in 1998, when they had come to his apartment, despite Taylor's protestations that in his heart of hearts, he knew Porter pulled the trigger, that he would not be happy until the day Porter died, and all he wanted was to be left alone. He also discussed it with Appolon Beaudouin earlier in 1997 and with Protess and Ciolino in 1998, when they came calling. He went over it during his 1999 grand jury appearance with Gainer. So here he was again, being deposed in 2002, nearly two decades after Porter's original 1983 criminal trial, this time giving testimony to Jones, again playing a starring role during a high point in Porter's journey through the local criminal justice system. Though testifying for Porter at the civil trial, Taylor hardly shaved the truth when questioned by Jones about what he saw the night of the pool shootings.

JONES: What did you see when you looked up after you heard the shot?

TAYLOR: I saw a man running down the bleachers past me. I saw a gun in his hand.

JONES: Now, the person that you saw running down the bleachers, as you sit here today, who was that person?

TAYLOR: It looked like Anthony Porter.

The nearly two-week-long trial ended on November 16, 2005, with the Montgomery team asking jurors to compensate their wrongfully convicted client to the tune of $24 million.

Following a day of deliberations, jurors filed back into Flannery's courtroom, took their seats, and—through the jury foreman—delivered a bombshell verdict that sent shock waves across the Windy City and beyond. Jurors found that neither the City nor Salvatore and Gray had acted maliciously, that the detectives had probable cause to arrest Porter, that Porter had not been abused by the police, and, because of those findings, they were not awarding the plaintiff a single penny.

It was a verdict that brought broad grins to the faces of Salvatore and Gray and high fives between them as Salvatore proclaimed, "We were vindicated.... We were vindicated." It shocked Porter family members and stunned his legal team. It set news pundits and beat reporters to handwringing and bellowing. Again, this was not supposed to be part of the script. This was not how it was to end.

In addition to howls of outrage, the media—and other Porter sympathizers—went through the weirdest contortions as they attempted to explain to their readers and viewers the trial's outcome.

"It is difficult to get inside the mechanization of the police force, and it is the police that control the facts," said Montgomery. "We are absolutely stunned," he added and also noted that there were no African-Americans on the jury.

The civil jury did not award damages to Porter and at the same time it did not offer commentary about his guilt or innocence as regards the original crime. The civil jury's verdict meant simply that the jury did not feel that Porter's rights had been violated at any point in the process. Yet for his supporters, it was as if he had been unjustly re-convicted, because determining that he had no claim for damages seemed to suggest that his 1983 murder conviction had, in fact, been appropriate.

Those who did not believe that Porter had been falsely imprisoned drew exactly the same conclusion—that the civil jury's decision in effect re-convicted Porter of the murders—but with an exactly opposite reaction. They argued that this was the third time that the facts about the 1982 murders at the Washington Park pool had been closely examined, and each time the facts pointed toward Porter's guilt.

First, he was convicted by the jury that found him guilty at his 1983 trial. The second time the evidence was examined was when the 1999 Gainer grand jury heard from six pool witnesses, all of whom put Porter in the pool area that night and five of whom implicated him directly or indirectly as being the killer. And now, a civil jury had ruled against him after having heard pretty much the same testimony as had been presented at the 1983 trial and the 1999 grand jury.

One of the strangest incidents in the entire Porter saga occurred moments after the verdict came in. Reporters rushed to Walter Jones and asked how such a verdict was possible. After all, an innocent man had been locked up for nearly two decades and once was fifty hours away from being put to death. For Jones, who, in preparing to defend the cops and the City, had read all the testimony and materials generated since the 1982 shootings, the answer was simplicity itself. "The killer," Jones said, standing in the doorway of Flannery's courtroom on the 26th floor of the Richard J. Daley Center, "has been sitting in that room right there all day." As he made that pronouncement, he pointed to the plaintiff's table in the well of the courtroom where Porter had been seated throughout the trial.

Jones delivered the uncomplicated explanation without any reporter asking the single most important follow-up question of the day: "Well, Mr. Jones, if in fact Porter was the killer, what on earth is Simon doing in Danville?"

The jury verdict triggered a most unusual Eric Zorn column that appeared on the front page of the *Tribune* on November 20. It began, "The City of Chicago doesn't owe Anthony Porter any money. But it owes him a big apology." Then after revisiting high points of what led to Porter's freedom in 1999, Zorn wrote:

> Porter spent 16 years on death row for that crime and was 50 hours

and 22 minutes away from a lethal injection before he was granted a reprieve based on a long-shot claim of mental incompetency.

Yet Tuesday, shortly after the jury's verdict was announced, Walter Jones, the attorney representing the City, pointed to the table in the courtroom where Porter sat during the trial and told *Tribune* reporter Charles Sheehan: "The killer has been sitting in that room right there all day." It was a stunning, graceless and infamous accusation.

Zorn had not once set foot in the courtroom during the two-week trial.

12

Justice
at Hand

Eleven days after Alstory Simon was sentenced and sent to Stateville Correctional Center in Crest Hill, Illinois, where he was being held temporarily before being transferred to Danville, he received a typed letter from his attorney Jack Rimland. Dated September 14, 1999, the letter left Simon in a state of near shock and boiling with rage. In it Rimland, by implication, made it clear that all bets were off, and that there was nothing more Rimland could or would do to help Simon with his case.

Addressed to the Stateville Correctional Center, Mr. Alstory Simon, Inmate No. K76376, P.O. Box 112, Joliet, IL 60403, Rimland, wrote, in part, "You pled guilty and were found guilty of Murder and were sentenced to thirty-seven years to be served in the Illinois Department of Corrections to run concurrent with the sentence given on the Voluntary Manslaughter. Additionally, you have been given two hundred and twelve days credit for time served.

"This correspondence confirms the conclusion of this matter. It has been a pleasure to represent you in this matter. I hope that your time goes well. Take Care."

It was signed, "Very Truly Yours, Jack P. Rimland."

After Protess and Ciolino refused to take his calls or respond

to his messages, it was all too evident that they too had no intention of carrying through with promises of only two years' incarceration followed by an abundance of riches upon his release.
So once he was permanently located at Danville, Alstory Simon
spent as much time as possible researching the law in the prison's library, specifically learning what constituted a post-conviction relief claim. And, on July 3, 2001, acting pro se, he filed his
first claim for post-conviction relief with the Cook County Circuit Court. It was no "Crayola petition." That is to say, it was well
written and well researched.

Its fifteen pages contain references to all the Rimland, Protess, Ciolino, and Gainer misrepresentations that have already
been examined. And Simon included his entire court file to create a foundation for his petition—files that had been forwarded
to him from the court clerk's office back in Cook County, portions
of which he referenced repeatedly.

On page one, the prisoner goes to the core of the wrongdoing,
writing:

> In the instant case, even though Petitioner Simon gave pleas of
> guilty at the Change of Plea Hearing and a statement of confession
> to the charges pending against him: said pleas of guilty and confes
> sion were involuntary where his free will was overborne by coercive
> actions and the unlawful promises used to "brainwash" him to obtain
> his compliance...while his counsel's inactive representation facilitat
> ed the scheme to compel petitioner to plead guilty and confess to the
> crimes he did not commit.

Simon's petition then takes a step-by-step journey through the
conspiracy that he felt Protess hatched. He describes how, in his
view, Gainer and Rimland withheld, distorted, and manufactured
evidence during the sentencing hearing, including the withhold-

ing of grand jury testimony inculpating Porter. He also relates the fact that Simon's illegal confession was extracted by an armed Ciolino with threats of physical harm, falsehoods, and promises that Protess, possessing great clout, would see that he only served two years.

Assistant State's Attorney Gainer and attorney Rimland knew but did not admonish the Court that Petitioner Simon's confession and pleas were the involuntary product of the coercion and promises used to obtain his cooperation to free Anthony Porter from death row and his imminent execution for the crimes now charged against Petitioner," the petition asserts.

To effect Petitioner's confession and his involuntary cooperation to free Anthony Porter from prison, State of Illinois investigator Paul Ciolino and his employee Arnold Reed used threats, sophisticated brainwashing techniques and monetary reward promises.

After referencing a synopsis of the grand jury testimony of the five witnesses who identified Porter as the triggerman, the petition charges that, after Ciolino and Reed admitted they were not actually police officers, they "informed Petitioner that they were working for Professor David Protess of Northwestern University and he would get him a lawyer and make sure that he would not spend more than a couple of years in prison. They indicated that they were not interested in seeing (Petitioner) do any time, they just wanted to get Anthony Porter off of death row."

Without appointment of counsel, Alstory Simon's petition was summarily denied by Cook County Circuit Court Judge Evelyn B. Clay on October 5, 2001, and her decision subsequently was upheld on appeal to the First Judicial District of Illinois.

By early 2006, however, attorneys Terry Ekl and Jim Sotos, along with their investigators Jimmy Delorto and Johnny Mazzola, were of the growing belief that the day was approaching when the Cook County state's attorney would grant them a request for a relief hearing on behalf of their imprisoned client. Their optimism this second time around was rooted in the fact that the second plea for relief contained powerful new evidence that had been unearthed by Delorto and Mazzola. After interviewing Inez Jackson informally and making a videotape of the conversation, the two agents received her approval to record a second, nearly identical videotaped recantation of her claim that Alstory Simon was guilty.

Two days after Christmas 2005, starting at 1:17 P.M., Inez Jackson commenced her second videotaped recantation, which was reduced to a 118-page transcript. Present at the videotaped recantation at her son Jim's house at 10308 Jonen Street in Milwaukee were Ekl; Cook County Assistant State's Attorney Celeste S. Stack; Bonnie H. Domask, a court reporter; and Owen May, the videographer. At that time, Sotos and Ekl considered Stack, a career prosecutor, an individual of profound integrity who was on their side in getting Simon a hearing. They absolutely believed that if Simon ever was to be exonerated, it would be owing in large part to Stack's understanding and assistance from the inside of State's Attorney Alvarez's office. Sotos and Ekl were wrong.

In the video Inez Jackson declares that she made her false allegations against Simon for three reasons: she had received promises from David Protess and Paul Ciolino of huge amounts of money that would come her way; Protess had assured her that he would secure the freedom of Walter Jackson, her nephew, and Sonny Jackson, her son, from the Illinois and Wisconsin penitentiaries, respectively, where both were serving sentences for murder; and she was angry with Simon, from whom she had been estranged for a decade.

Inez was fifty-five-years old at the time of the second video. She was skin and bones—ravaged by AIDS, suffering from emphysema, attached to an oxygen tank, and lying prone on a couch on the upper floor of her son's Milwaukee house. Her sunken eyes darted about as she coughed and wheezed, a bandanna wrapped around her head. In truth, Inez was very near death—she would live for only a few weeks after the video session.

It is clear that the woman tossing and turning on the videotape was fighting for her life, for every breath, as she explained why she falsely identified her husband as the killer in the January 29, 1999, video taken by Ciolino in Shawn Armbrust's Brookfield, Wisconsin, home. To repeat, her response, in a nutshell, was this: Protess was writing a book, and she would get a lot of money from the proceeds of its sale. In addition, Protess would somehow dramatically reduce the life prison sentences of her son and her nephew. But she first had to incriminate Simon, with whom she was angry and from whom she had been estranged for a decade.

Ekl began the questioning, asking Inez about the events surrounding the August 15, 1982, pool shootings. She and Alstory had been in the park with the victims, she said, "they were drinking," but she and Al returned home around 10 P.M., via an ice cream parlor where they ordered a couple of ice cream cones. After arriving home, they remained there for the rest of the night. Hillard and Green—whom Inez described as a close friend whose children Inez babysat—stayed behind in the park.

"Was Simon responsible for the shootings?" Ekl wanted to know.

"No," came the reply.

"Was Alstory Simon present at the time of the shootings?" Ekl asked.

"No," Inez responded.

"Was he in the bleachers at the time?"

"No."

Then Ekl questioned Inez at length about a Protess ploy that

was used in the Ford Heights Four case and had been used elsewhere since. Namely, offers of money, lots of it, to key witnesses
in exchange for altered testimony, but only if the new testimony
advanced Protess's goals.

EKL: Did Professor Protess say he might write a book?

INEZ: No, he said he was going to write a book.

EKL: Did he tell you that you were going to get something out
of that?

INEZ: Yes.

EKL: What did he tell you, you would get?

INEZ: He didn't say how much, but he [say] just for the signature [on the affidavit Protess had prepared for her to sign]. I had
to sign it first and then get some money and then wait for the rest.

EKL: He told you that if you signed off on something that you
would get the money?

INEZ: Yes.

EKL: And was there then talk about I think you said getting
some money from Anthony Porter when he got out?

INEZ: Yes.

EKL: What were you told about that?

INEZ: That Anthony Porter was going to give me a lot of money
for setting him free.

EKL: Do you know if it was Protess or Ciolino that made that
statement?

INEZ: I don't know which one it was.

EKL: One of the two though?

INEZ: Yes.

Ekl then shifted his line of questioning about how Inez obtained
her lawyer, Martin Abrams, who would represent her for being an
accessory to the crime and, ultimately, get that charge dismissed.

EKL: Now, somebody arranged for you to have a lawyer in connection with this case?

INEZ: Yes.

EKL: Do you know if Paul Ciolino and David Protess arranged for you to have a lawyer, Martin Abrams?

INEZ: Yes.

EKL: Did you have to pay Mr. Abrams?

INEZ: No.

Finally, Ekl asks Inez why she is now recanting earlier testimony in which she alleged that her husband was the killer.

INEZ: Because I don't want to die carrying it to my grave.

EKL: You didn't want to die carrying it to your grave?

INEZ: Yes, knowing that Alstory was innocent.

EKL: Knowing that Alstory was an innocent man?

INEZ: Yes.

When questioned by Celeste Stack, Inez painted a portrait of Alstory Simon that was far different from the one that emerged in 1999 when Simon appeared before Judge Fitzgerald, pleaded guilty, and apologized to Marilyn Green's mother and the victim's two children. Inez said she had five grown children of her own—none with Alstory—and Alstory was like a father to them all: Tiffany, Sonny, Alvin, Mike, and Ediss. But, Inez said, he was especially close to Tiffany.

"Did he ever strike the kids?" Stack wanted to know.

"No," Inez answered.

Was she scared of Alstory Simon?

That Stack question went directly to the heart of all those who attempted to explain why Inez for so many years would keep silent about the double homicide she had witnessed. During all those years, from 1982 until 1999, there had been not a peep about that dreadful occurrence. Why? Protess and the others had the answer. They would tell the skeptics that it was fear of Simon's retribution that caused Inez to keep her mouth shut.

Her answer to Stack's question? No, she was not afraid of Simon. Was she still married to him? Yes. Were they living together? No, they had been separated for ten years following a nasty argument, but they had seen each other on occasion. She had known Alstory since the first grade; they attended high school together. Had Alstory ever struck Inez? Once, the woman said, but she deserved it. Did she know Marilyn, the victim? Yes, she was her best friend.

Had Inez heard from Alstory Simon since he was imprisoned? Yes, Inez replied, about two months earlier, in a letter he had sent her from Danville. Did he ask you for help in getting him out of prison? Stack asked the woman, as Inez shifted on the couch, catching her breath, coughing. "No, he never asked me for help. Just wanted to know how the kids were doing. He wanted to know how I was doing. How the kids were doing. Especially Tiffany," Inez said. He was very close to Tiffany, but he loved all the kids.

"So," Stack asked, "why are you now recanting your earlier statement?"

The reply was the same that Inez gave Ekl: "Because I do not want to die going to my grave knowing that Alstory Simon was innocent."

Following more questions from Stack, Inez explained how her interaction with Protess unfolded through a series of phone calls and a visit to her Milwaukee home. She said Walter called her from Danville prison to tell her that he had talked to Protess and that Protess asked him to call her and tell her to lie about Alstory's involvement. After she said she agreed to the scheme, Protess, Ciolino, and "two white girls" showed up at her house a few days later. That was on January 29, 1999, the day she signed the affidavit and engaged in the videotaping.

In her November 11, 2005, recantation, Inez says that in 1999 she received a phone call from her nephew Walter. "Walter was in the penitentiary and he told me that it would help him if he helped Anthony Porter beat the case. He also gave me some facts on how the murders were supposed to have happened," in order to give her testimony a greater sense of validity.

A final note. Stack took Inez Jackson through a copy of her four-page affidavit, which Protess had written and Inez had signed in 1999. Stack pointed out more than a dozen instances where the document had been altered and the initials, MIS, as in Margaret Inez Simon, purporting to be Inez's, had been inserted to indicate that Inez had approved the alterations in the document. As they went over the initialed portions, each time Stack asked whether in fact Inez had been responsible for the initials. Inez pointed to at least a dozen instances, calling the "signatures" forgeries.

"Those aren't my initials," the bedridden woman repeated, several times. "They are too neat."

Nonetheless, Celeste Stack, the long-serving assistant state's attorney, departed the December 27, 2005, Inez questioning session saying she did not find it "compelling." Ekl, Sotos, and the two former ATF agents were dumbfounded.

Inez's recantation was accompanied by three affidavits signed by Inez, her nephew Walter Jackson, and her son Sonny Jackson. The affidavits had been obtained by Delorto and Mazzola. In them, Inez, Walter, and Sonny describe how they believe they had been misled by Protess to further his scheme to free Porter. In his January 6, 2006, affidavit, Sonny, who was incarcerated in the Stanley Correctional Center in Stanley, Wisconsin, recanted his original affidavit, which had contained equally compelling testimony against Alstory Simon. In the 2006 recantation document, Sonny declares, "I do not know who shot and killed those people, but I do know that my mother could not have been there and was not a witness to the crime."

The last paragraph says, "Later, sometime around November 2001, my mother told me that people from Northwestern Uni-

versity named Ciolino and Professor Protess promised her a lot
of money if she would help them by saying that she saw Alstory
Simon kill Marilyn Green and Jerry Hillard."

On January 19, 2006, Delorto and Mazzola obtained a second
recantation, this one from Walter Jackson, who was serving a long
sentence in the Illinois River Correctional Center in Canton, Illinois, at the time. His one-page, thirteen-paragraph account is
straightforward, powerful, and leaves nothing to the imagination.

> In late 1998, while at Danville, I received a letter from Professor
> David Protess. The letter asked me to call him at his home. I called
> Professor Protess at his home and he told me that if I helped him free
> Anthony Porter that he would help me get out of jail.
>
> He told me that he wanted me to get the cooperation of Inez Jack-
> son. Professor Protess also made some statement about there being
> money waiting for me when I got out. I told him I would do whatever
> he wanted.

Next to last, Jackson asserts:

> In January of 1999 while I was incarcerated at the Danville Correc-
> tional Center I was visited by students who were working with Profes-
> sor David Protess. When they came to visit me they had a statement
> for me to sign.... Alstory Simon never told me that he shot Jerry and
> Marilyn. I signed this statement because Professor Protess promised
> to help me get out of jail.

And lastly, Jackson writes:

> The students working for Professor Protess also asked me to call
> Inez Jackson, asking her to help Porter beat his case. I spoke on the
> phone to both Inez Jackson and her daughter, Tiffany, and told both

of them that if Inez helped Professor Protess and the students get Porter out of jail, then Professor Protess was going to help me. I asked her to do whatever they asked because I believed that it was going to help me get out of jail.

The January 19, 2006, affidavit is signed by Walter Jackson and witnessed by James Delorto and John J. Mazzola.

Eight to nine months later, despite the astonishing new evidence and the dying declaration of Inez, Cook County Criminal Court Judge Evelyn Clay, in a fourteen-page order, issued her response to the Ekl/Sotos request for a post-conviction hearing based on that new evidence. It was a request that had been vigorously contested by Cook County State's Attorney Dick Devine.

"Petitioner has failed to show that a substantial violation of his rights occurred," Judge Clay wrote. "The State's Motion to Dismiss petitioner's successive post-conviction petition is granted."

———————

At about the same time Judge Clay dismissed the Ekl/Sotos petition, Porter, who was now fifty-one-years-old and apparently had kept his nose clean since the March 2000 beating of Carlia Perkins, found himself jammed up a second time. On November 30, 2006, Porter was indicted by a Kankakee County grand jury. He was charged with assaulting Tracy Bell, twenty-eight, his girlfriend and mother of five of his children. Specifically, he struck her in the face with a beer bottle until it shattered, slicing through her right cheek.

Porter fled the scene but later was arrested, charged with felony domestic abuse, and jailed in the Jerome Combs Detention Center in Kankakee, unable to make the $25,000 bail. Bell, battered and bleeding, was taken by ambulance to Provena St. Mary's Hospital in Kankakee where she required forty stitches.

The assault charge stemmed from a 911 call police received around 3 A.M. on November 22, 2006. When police arrived at the Bell home, the woman told police that Porter, who had fled through a window in the apartment, had struck her following an altercation while they were playing cards at a friend's house nearby.

Kankakee Police Investigations Commander Larry Osenga said Bell told authorities, "They were drinking and he [Porter] made a request of her, she didn't reply quickly enough, so he battered her with a beer bottle. The bottle broke and she received several cuts."

In June 2007, Porter pleaded guilty to a Class A misdemeanor offense of resisting arrest and was sentenced to two years conditional discharge and fined $300.

There was little coverage from the press following this latest episode of raw violence.

13

A Crossroads

In 2006, two events took place inside Medill's Fisk Hall that would profoundly impact the renowned journalism school and lead ultimately to the end of David Protess's career as a journalism instructor, at least at Northwestern. The first event was a simple change of personnel. John Lavine was installed as Medill dean, replacing the outgoing Ken Bode who had headed Medill during a rocky two-and-a-half year stewardship in which, among other criticisms, he was accused by students of favoring broadcast journalism courses over traditional print media instruction. The second event directly involved Protess, who was winding up a long-term investigation into another wrongful murder conviction that had taken place nearly three decades earlier in south-suburban Harvey.

First, Lavine. He was no newcomer to Northwestern. A Carleton College graduate, Lavine had been associated with Northwestern's Kellogg School of Business for more than fifteen years and was a founder in 1989 of Northwestern University's Media Management Center, which, among other objectives, educates senior media executives in the latest trends in management. Nor was he a newcomer to the world of publishing. Before arriving on the lakefront campus, he had spent more than two decades as publisher and editor of four daily and four weekly newspapers in Wisconsin.

When Lavine was selected to head Medill, Northwestern President Henry Bienen and Provost Lawrence Dumas suspended formal faculty oversight of the new incoming dean and ceded authority to him to effect sweeping changes in the journalism school's curriculum. And Lavine did just that, creating what he called the "Medill 2020 Plan," an initiative that triggered immediate angst among many of Medill's veteran professors.

Under the transformed curriculum, multimedia and marketing components were integrated into many classes, creating fear and anger among longtime staffers that the new approach could lead to a breach of the sacred wall that had separated journalists from the world of advertising and marketing. Medill professor Michelle Weldon, who collaborated with Lavine on the new course design starting in 2005, defended the broad changes. "We fundamentally changed how the early courses were taught," she said, noting that the new curriculum introduced multimedia and audience analysis components to the introductory courses. "There was so much resistance. He got so much criticism by discussing audiences at all. So many people said journalists need to be pure, and this is pandering. But it's not pandering. It's survival." The latter was a reference by Weldon to the profound and negative impact the Internet was having on traditional media outlets.

Regardless, the change was met with angry resistance.

The following year, with the bad aroma of Medill 2020 still lingering in the air, things only got more uncomfortable for Lavine when a second major controversy erupted. Dubbed "Quotegate," its origins can be traced to the dean himself. In spring 2007 Lavine had penned an article for *Northwestern,* the University's alumni magazine, in which he quoted unnamed students heaping praise on a course titled Advertising: Building Brand Name, which was one of the new classes that had been ushered in by Lavine's Medill 2020 plan.

Student journalist David Spett, who had read Lavine's essay, was struck by one of the anonymous quotes in particular because he thought it odd, not sounding like something a student would say, according to one account. A second more widely accepted version, championed in an October 20, 2011, story by the *Chicago Reader,* claimed that Spett had been tipped off to the suspect quote by Protess, whose relationship with his new boss had been frosty almost from day one. According to the *Reader* article, Protess urged Spett to investigate the veracity of the quote.

Lavine's essay has the unnamed student exclaiming, "I came to Medill because I want to inform people and make things better. Journalism is the best way for me to do that, but I sure felt good about this class. It is one of the best I've taken, and I learned many things in it that apply as much to truth-telling in journalism as to this campaign to save teenage drivers."

A Medill senior at the time, Spett obtained the twenty-seven-student class roster and asked each student in the class—all juniors—if they'd said such a thing. They all said no. He then published a story in the *Daily Northwestern* that accused Lavine of making up the quote, in part to defend the curriculum changes his leadership had effected and to clothe those changes in some sort of legitimacy.

Following publication of the Spett piece, Protess went on the offensive. He introduced a faculty motion calling on Lavine to reveal his sources. Lavine responded, incredulously given his background and position, by saying that identifying the source was an impossibility because he had thrown away his notes and erased relevant e-mails from his office computer.

In the brouhaha's aftermath, Protess took a second direct, public shot at his boss. "Medill faculty teach our students that journalism should be transparent. It is a mistake when I don't set the best example I can." Protess added, "I would flunk a student who did what the dean did."

Subsequently, university provost Daniel Linzer appointed three prominent Medill graduates, including former *Chicago Tribune* publisher Jack Fuller, to investigate the Quotegate matter. After the panel completed its review, Linzer announced that it had uncovered "no evidence to point to any likelihood that the quotes were fabricated."

Linzer added, "The committee unanimously concluded that although a record of the student statements that were quoted cannot be found, sufficient material does exist about the relevant storefront reporting experience and marketing course to demonstrate that sentiments similar to the quotes had been expressed by students. Thus, the committee found that there is ample evidence that the quotes were consistent with sentiments students expressed about the course in course evaluations and no evidence to point to any likelihood that the quotes were fabricated."

Following the Linzer announcement, the *Tribune* published an editorial broadside in which it asserted that Linzer had issued a "mush-mouth" statement. The newspaper said Lavine had fabricated "self-serving lies," adding that, "there is indeed evidence suggesting that the quotations were fabricated: Spett's research."

Lavine survived the double body blows, which had been widely reported, and by 2008, the negative headwinds triggered by Quotegate and arising from the Medill 2020 initiative had abated significantly. For Protess, on the other hand, the headwinds were just beginning to blow, and by early 2009, they would turn into a virtual gale. To appreciate the storm Protess was facing and where it would take him, a brief history is valuable.

With the onset of the fall 2003 quarter, Protess and his students had discovered what they suspected was another prisoner who had been wrongly convicted of murder. This time it was the so-called McKinney Case. The Medill investigation began on a quiet note, but over the next three years, as the McKinney Case was successively passed off from one group of outgoing students to a new group of incoming students, quarter after quarter, it would eventually generate once again a round of dramatic headlines. This time, however, the blaring headlines would be drastically less friendly to Protess than those associated with the Anthony Porter saga.

The facts of the McKinney Case are these. On the night of September 15, 1978, a white security guard named Donald Lundahl was killed by a shotgun blast at close range while he sat in his car outside a Masonic Temple in the Chicago suburb of Harvey. Later that evening a man named Anthony McKinney, an African-American, was arrested after police spotted him running down the street. McKinney, eighteen at the time, was unarmed and had no criminal history.

He was briefly released after telling police he had been watching the Muhammad Ali–Leon Spinks heavyweight championship fight when the murder took place, and he was running from gang-bangers when the arresting officer spotted him. Authorities questioned another teenager, who told police that he saw the murder, claiming that he heard McKinney, from fifty yards away, say, "Your money or your life," and shoot Lundahl. McKinney was arrested a second time, signed a confession, recanted his confession during his trial, but was convicted nevertheless by a jury and sentenced to life in prison.

Beginning with the 2003 fall quarter and ending with the spring 2006 quarter, the McKinney Case remained a central, unrelenting focus of Protess and the Innocence Project. A succession of nine sets of Medill students worked the case and over time developed evidence that proved McKinney was not guilty of the decades-old Lundahl murder.

Nicole Lapin, a former CNBC and CNN Live anchor and founder of Nothing but Gold Productions, which produces accessible financial content across multiple platforms, is a Medill graduate who worked on the McKinney Case while enrolled for two quarters in Protess's class in 2009. She wrote a November 6, 2009, description of the cutting-edge, new evidence the Medill team had uncovered. Her piece was written for CNN where she was employed at the time.

> In our investigation we re-enacted the crime scene and determined it was impossible to discern any words spoken or shouted from 50 yards away. Later, we tracked down the then-teenage witness who said he saw McKinney that night. The man recanted his testimony on videotape, and told us police beat him.
>
> We also found a fire department document that indicated the paramedics were called to the police station during McKinney's interrogation, raising the question of whether he was roughed up during his interrogation as he said he was.
>
> We interviewed the gangbangers who chased him that night. They acknowledged they chased him after the Ali fight because they were angry he had damaged their car earlier. Finally, we identified alternate suspects, one of whom stated on videotape that he was there when the murder was committed—and that McKinney wasn't.

By 2008, the Innocence Project, which had by then ended its review of the McKinney Case, was in possession of a small mountain of materials in the form of e-mails, memos, copies of relevant court files, taped interviews, and more. Some of those materials had been shared with Karen Daniels, a graduate of Harvard Law School, a former member of the Illinois Office of the State Appel-

late Defender, and a staff attorney at the Center on Wrongful
Convictions, soon to become its co-director. In spring 2008, she
and Steven Drizin, another Wrongful Convictions lawyer, filed
a petition with Cook County Criminal Court Judge Dianne Cannon seeking a McKinney retrial based on new evidence dug up
by the Innocence Project and by their own center.

The new evidence included allegations that McKinney's signed
confession in the case was obtained by intimidation, threats, and
beatings. Two eyewitnesses, Dennis Pettis and Wayne Phillips,
who told Harvey police that they witnessed the 1978 shooting,
had by 2008 recanted.

Meanwhile there was a side issue playing out in 2008 that
had nothing to do with the Cannon court proceedings and everything to do with Lavine and Protess. To some extent, it remains
obscured in a misty haze, yet it deserves mention. In early 2008,
Lavine asked Eric Ferkenhoff, a former _Tribune_ reporter who had
become a Medill lecturer, to do a pedagogical study of Protess's
investigative reporting class, following the professor around, sitting in on his lectures, and interviewing his students and individuals associated with his investigations.

After all, Protess was a Medill star, a master at digging out the
truth, and his skills should be shared with colleagues. To that end,
when Ferkenhoff was finished with his reporting, he would write
a comprehensive report, plumbing Protess's reporting methodol-
ogies, a report that would then be shared with Medill professors
and students, providing the latter group with valuable guidance
on how to get to the bottom of things.

Initially, Protess was flattered by the idea but soon soured on
it. Word was getting back to Protess from individuals Ferkenhoff
had interviewed, suggesting that by the sound of his questions,
Ferkenhoff wasn't one bit interested in Protess's reporting meth-
odologies. Ferkenhoff seemed to be out to discredit the professor,

presumably at Lavine's direction. In November 2008, Protess's attorney, Robert Stephenson, wrote Lavine a letter accusing Ferkenhoff of using "false promises and misrepresentations" to gather information "aimed at unjustifiably discrediting" Protess and the Innocence Project. The letter threatened a lawsuit.

Ferkenhoff never completed his pedagogical paper, but he did hire an attorney to look out for his interests should Protess—or anyone else, for that matter—try to come after him seeking his sources or notes. Moreover, Ferkenhoff was taking no chances because his attorney of record was Sheldon T. Zenner, national co-head of litigation and dispute resolution at Chicago's Katten Muchin Rosenman LLP, an upper-echelon, powerhouse Chicago law firm.

Though Zenner advised Ferkenhoff to keep his mouth shut, the Medill lecturer did put out a limited statement denying that he was being used as a tool by anybody to get Protess.

> As for being used, the answer, to me, is simple: No. Was I ever worried? Of course. People were saying off things about Protess and I wondered whose agenda was at play. That's part of our job as journalists—to figure that out and still come straight.
>
> In the end, I did my job. Straight. I did not believe—nor do I now—that the dean or any of his deputies set off on some campaign to bring an end to David Protess's career. I don't believe I had anything to do with him leaving the school. That was a decision between him and the school, and I know no details about it. I don't want to.
>
> To believe I took part in this alleged campaign to end Protess's career after nearly 30 years is to believe I was duped and too stupid to realize it; or a flat tool who engaged in it knowingly.

As the on-again, off-again McKinney hearings dragged on before

Judge Cannon, Cook County State's Attorney Anita Alvarez, a career prosecutor, and her assistants, led by Celeste Stack, head of Alvarez's Conviction Integrity Unit, grew increasingly skeptical about claims of McKinney's innocence. After the Cook County State's Attorney's office started reinvestigating the case, prosecutors raised questions about the students' methods. "When we went out and interviewed these people, we were finding that they were telling us, you know, 'No, that's not what I said to them,' or, 'This is what they said to me, this is how that statement came about,'" Alvarez said.

Prosecutors also harbored suspicions about what Medill investigative materials had or had not been turned over to the defense, and they suggested in court filings that students had lied about their identities, flirted with potential witnesses, sometimes even paid them in exchange for information that squared with their view of the McKinney case. Prosecutors further suggested that students may have been so driven to get an 'A' in the class that they twisted or suppressed evidence in their cause to free McKinney.

With that, in May 2009 Alvarez turned the tables on Protess, Medill, and Northwestern University, and things really heated up. Her office served a court-approved subpoena on Medill that was sweeping indeed. The subpoena sought eleven categories of documents relating to the McKinney case—student grades and grading criteria, evaluations of student performance, expenses incurred during the inquiry, the course syllabus, e-mails, unpublished student memos, and interviews not conducted on the record or where witnesses weren't willing to be recorded.

The subpoena drew swift reactions from media watchdogs. The state's attorney's office was instantly accused of overreaching and bringing an icy chill to press freedoms. Observers were dismayed that Anita Alvarez seemed to be calling into question the integrity of one of the nation's leading journalism schools.

"The only reason I can think that the prosecutors would issue such a broad subpoena is to take down the program," said Don Craven, the interim executive director of the Illinois Press Association and an expert on libel and First Amendment law.

Phyllis Goldfarb, the Jacob Burns Foundation Professor of Clinical Law at George Washington University, also reacted negatively. "It is highly unusual. It's hard to understand the motive for a subpoena that is this broad. This is an investigative journalism class at a major university," she said. "One of the fundamental themes of any journalism class is integrity and objectivity, so the innuendo that the [state's attorney] would find something in these documents that would say a student was offered an 'A' if they found the man innocent is an attack on the integrity of the institution."

Alvarez's office had a different interpretation of the subpoena. "At the end of the day, all we're seeking is the same thing these students are: justice and truth," said Sally Daly, Alvarez's spokesperson. Daly said the prosecutors wished to see all statements the students received from witnesses, whether they supported or contradicted the notion of McKinney's innocence.

"We're not trying to delve into areas of privacy or grades," Ms. Daly said. "Our position is that they've engaged in an investigative process, and without any hostility, we're seeking to get all of the information they've developed, just as detectives and investigators turn over."

Based on Protess representations that he had shared only limited materials with the Daniels team, the university dug in its heels. Richard O'Brien, a partner at Sidley & Austin LLP, a leading law firm headquartered in Chicago, represented Northwestern in its fight to limit the scope of the Alvarez request.

O'Brien's core argument: While a small amount of materials may have been shared with the defense, those limited materials would be made available to prosecutors. Relying on Protess representations, O'Brien further argued that the vast bulk of investigative materials had not been given to the defense, and since the students were reporters, they were protected by Illinois's shield law from having to surrender the remaining investigative documents to third parties, most notably more than 500 e-mails that had been generated internally.

For Protess the beginning of the end came in the fall of 2010. O'Brien, whose firm had been paid $500,000 up to that point, accused the professor of giving him inaccurate information about what investigative notes had been turned over to McKinney's lawyers. "We believe that you have displayed a lack of candor with us and have not cooperated with us," O'Brien wrote Protess in an e-mail shortly before withdrawing from the case.

Without an attorney on the case and facing a ballooning public relations nightmare, not to mention legal liability, Northwestern University then hired Anton Valukas, a former U.S. Attorney in Chicago and Chairman of Jenner & Block, one of the leading criminal defense law firms in the country. Jenner & Block investigators promptly set about conducting an internal investigation of Protess and the Innocence Project, which included forensic analyses of the hard drives on Protess's home and office computers.

By the following spring, Protess's fate had been sealed. As the Valukas investigation unfolded, and its initial findings began to spell trouble for Protess, the twenty-nine-year journalism professor was informed in mid-March 2011 that he would not be teaching his Investigative Reporting course that spring quarter. Instead, Protess was informed via an e-mail from Senior Director of Undergraduate Education Michele Bitoun, that Alec Klein, an award-winning, former investigative reporter for the *Washington Post,* would be teaching the class.

On April 6, 2011, the boom came down. That was the day Lavine chaired a two-hour, closed-door, frequently stormy meeting of all Medill faculty members—all but Protess, who was barred from attending. Using a PowerPoint presentation that had been put together by Jenner & Block, the dean detailed how a review of Protess's conduct had led to his decision not only to remove Protess from teaching that spring quarter but to place him on leave as well. The meeting was riven right down the middle. On one side were those who revered Protess for his work in exonerating the innocent; some charged that Lavine was settling a personal score with Protess for his role in Quotegate. On the other side were those who consistently had viewed Protess's investigative methods with a jaded eye.

But for some who followed the history of Protess and the Medill Innocence Project, their parting of ways was not surprising. Former students and colleagues painted a picture of Protess as an individual whose abrasive and egotistical personality got in the way of his unassailable intentions and obvious talents. That personality, combined with success in freeing convicted individuals, earned the professor enemies in law enforcement, local government, and even the Medill faculty. It also led Protess to push the boundaries of acceptable classroom activities.

Some critics ascribed the Protess transgressions to a complete lack of oversight. Jennifer Merritt, a former Protess student, is one such critic. "When you're allowed to run a program without any real oversight, this is the kind of thing that happens," she said. "Something is going to go wrong, somebody is going to cross the line, and you're really going to lose your credibility."

Meanwhile, only minutes after the explosive April 6 Lavine meeting, Alan K. Cubbage, Vice President, University Relations, released a lengthy statement detailing Protess's wrongdoing. It began:

Northwestern University generally does not discuss publicly actions regarding its faculty and staff. However, statements in the media by Professor David Protess and our desire to be as forthcoming as possible on an issue of great importance to the University, its faculty, our students, alumni and our community prompt us to make the following statement.

Jenner & Block scrutinized relevant material obtained from computer hard drives related to the McKinney matter and conducted interviews with individuals with first-hand knowledge of the conduct regarding the subpoenas in this case.

Cubbage then enumerated the findings of the Jenner & Block review:

- To be responsive to the subpoena, Northwestern needed to be certain which materials could be protected by a claim of reporter's privilege under Illinois law and not be relinquished to the State, and what materials would have to be turned over because they had been published or shared with a third party outside Medill. University lawyers repeatedly made the distinction clear to Protess, as the long-time Director of the Innocence Project, regarding what had been shared outside Medill and for which privilege could therefore not be claimed. Based on the information provided by Protess, the University took the position that student memos were privileged.

- In June 2010, the University discovered that there were many inconsistencies emerging between Protess's representations and the facts. Mr. McKinney's lawyers produced in court student memos they said were received from Protess or from the Medill Innocence Project at his direction—documents Protess had said were never shared outside Medill. As a result, it became clear that the position the University had taken in court concerning the students' memos was not supportable.

- The review uncovered considerable evidence that Protess authorized the release of all student memos to Mr. McKinney's lawyers despite his repeated claims to the contrary; knew from the very beginning that doing so waived any claim of privilege; and repeatedly provided false and misleading information to the lawyers and the dean. As just one example, in December 2009 Protess sent them a falsified communication in an attempt to hide the fact that the student memos had been shared with Mr. McKinney's lawyers. This communication included what Protess said was a copy of a November 2007 e-mail, unredacted save for removal of "personal information," that he had sent to his program assistant. The e-mail copy he provided stated that: "My position about memos, as you know, is that we don't keep copies...." However, examination of the original 2007 e-mail, which was only recently obtained by the University, revealed that the original wording actually was: "My position about memos, as you know, is that we share everything with the legal team, and don't keep copies...."

- In sum, Protess knowingly misrepresented the facts and his actions to the University, its attorneys and the dean of Medill on many documented occasions. He also misrepresented facts about these matters to students, alumni, the media and the public. He caused the University to take on what turned out to be an unsupportable case and unwittingly misrepresent the situation both to the Court and to the State.

In April 2011, Alec Klein succeeded Protess as director of the Medill Innocence Project, soon to be renamed the Medill Justice Project. Under the new leadership, the Justice Project revamped its operations across the board, instituting new policies and procedures and overhauling its website and introducing investigative articles, videos, podcasts and other multimedia, social media, and a series of other innovations, including a toning down of aggressive reporting techniques that had been a hallmark feature of Protess's approach to getting to the truth.

With Klein's guidance, the Medill Justice Project got off to an admirable start, earning nationwide recognition for its investigations, including two prestigious Peter Lisagor Awards from the Chicago chapter of the Society of Professional Journalists, a national award from Investigative Reporters and Editors, and a Sunshine Award from the National Society of Professional Journalists.

On September 7, 2011, Judge Cannon agreed with the state's attorney and ordered Medill to turn over more than 500 e-mails to prosecutors. In ordering Medill to surrender the e-mails, the judge concluded that the students had "worked at the direction of Anthony McKinney's attorneys" and acted "as investigators in a criminal proceeding, thereby losing the legal protections afforded independent journalists."

In August 2012, John Lavine, Dean of Northwestern University's Medill School of Journalism, Media, Integrated Marketing Communications, stepped down after a six-year stewardship. He said he planned to work on a project "examining how the media can determine if people are truly informed by the content they provide and seeking out new ways for the news media to remain viable."

On September 1, 2012, Bradley Hamm, former dean of the journalism school at Indiana University, with a doctorate in mass communication research from the University of North Carolina and a master's degree in journalism from the University of South Carolina, who had been appointed Lavine's successor, officially took the Medill reins.

On August 24, 2013, Anthony McKinney died in prison at age fifty-three.

14

The Pressure Builds

Protess's ignominious firing notwithstanding, the push on State's Attorney Alvarez to order a formal review of Simon's case had not diminished. In fact, it had increased exponentially. The professor's departure from Northwestern University and the reasons for it served to validate the positions taken by Delorto and Mazzola years earlier, and it likewise supported the increasing pressure from Sotos and Ekl. His departure validated the claims that had been outlined in "Chimera" and the central storyline spelled out in *Murder in the Park,* the Shawn Rech documentary that was nearing completion.

If Cook County prosecutors believed that with a little hunkering down and a little passage of time things would blow over, they were in for a big jolt. Not one big jolt, but two. The first arrived on September 20, 2013, when an affidavit signed by Thomas Edward Epach, the former chief of the Criminal Division when Simon was sentenced, was unveiled. It was stunning in its candor and its specificity. It was the document that Sotos, Ekl, and the retired ATF agents had been seeking for many months, something just short of their Holy Grail.

The Epach affidavit spells out in detail the bizarre, hopelessly conflicted, unethical and unprofessional manner in which Simon was railroaded and a man guilty of the two homicides was freed and subsequently pardoned on March 19, 1998, by Illinois Governor George Ryan.

The Epach affidavit is compelling. It also presents an indictment of Dick Devine and top assistants. It is quoted at length.

The undersigned, under oath, states as follows:

From December 1995 to April 2001, I was the Chief of the Criminal Division of the Cook County State's Attorney's Office under the elected State's Attorney, Richard Devine.

In late 1998, I was personally involved in representing the Cook County State's Attorney's Office in connection with a clemency petition filed by Anthony Porter who had been convicted of the murders of Jerry Hillard and Marilyn Green on August 15, 1982.

On February 3, 1999, a video was released to the media which purported to be a confession by Alstory Simon to the murders of Hillard and Green. The video was made by Paul Ciolino who was known to me to be working with David Protess in an effort to free Anthony Porter.

At the time the video was released, no one in the Cook County State's Attorney's Office had any information to establish the authenticity of this video.

Less than two days after the video of the alleged confession was broadcast by the media, State's Attorney Richard Devine made the decision to release Mr. Porter from custody. At the time this decision was made no one from the State's Attorney's Office had received a copy of the original video which purported to contain the confession of Alstory Simon.

In my years of experience as a prosecutor, it is my opinion that it was highly unusual, if not unprecedented, to make a decision to release an individual convicted of murder based upon the broadcast of a video, the reliability and authenticity of which had not been thoroughly investigated and established.

At the time of the release of Mr. Porter, I was aware not only that the purported confession of Alstory Simon was obtained by Paul Ciolino, who was working on behalf of Anthony Porter, but also that Simon was being represented by attorney Jack Rimland, who had close ties to both Mr. Ciolino and David Protess.

I believed at the time that the circumstances of this purported confession needed to be thoroughly investigated before a decision was made to either release Porter or to charge Simon with the crime.

I was also aware that there were substantial credible evidence to support the conviction of Anthony Porter and that no physical evidence existed which tied Simon to these murders.

Nevertheless, a decision was made by Mr. Devine to immediately release Porter and to charge Simon with the murders of Hillard and Green.

Following the release of Porter and the charging of Simon I was in charge of the presentation of evidence to a Cook County Grand Jury relating to the murders of Hillard and Green. The presentation was made at my direction by Assistant State's Attorney Thomas Gainer.

In his affidavit Epach then discusses the February 1999 grand jury in some detail, especially evidence that Gainer elicited from the four pool witnesses, Eugene Beckwith, Mark Senior, Kenneth Edwards, and William Taylor, testimony in which the four identify Porter as the gunman. But Epach goes further. He reprises the testimony of the late Henry Williams and Taylor, star witnesses during Porter's 1983 trial, and that of Anthony Liace, the Chicago policeman who stopped and frisked Porter as he raced from the pool.

Epach closes with a strongly worded rebuke of Devine.

Based upon the quality and quantity of evidence indicating the involvement of Anthony Porter in the murders of Hillard and Green, the sworn testimony at trial and the sworn testimony procured by the February 1999 grand jury, the involvement of Paul Ciolino in obtaining the purported confession and representation of Simon by an attorney with ties to Ciolino and Protess, I believed that questions remained about the guilt of Simon and the innocence of Porter that needed to be investigated.

I expressed these concerns to Mr. Devine. Subsequently I was told that the decision to prosecute Alstory Simon had been made by Mr. Devine.

Based upon the above, I have remaining reservations concerning the guilt of Alstory Simon for the murders of Hillard and Green. I believe the interest of Justice requires that Alstory Simon be given a full hearing during which he is clearly being represented by attorneys whose sole concern is in his best interest.

Further the Affiant sayeth naught.

Signed Thomas E. Epach Jr.

Then the second jolt arrived. It was a ten-page letter sent from Sotos and Ekl addressed to The Honorable Anita Alvarez, on October 8, 2013. The document is the first comprehensive distillate of key elements of Alstory Simon's railroading and of Medill meddling in criminal cases in addition to Simon's.

The Sotos/Ekl letter included a recapitulation of all that was in error about Simon's case, much of which already has been noted. But it was particularly damning of Rimland, Simon's lawyer. "Rimland never actually represented Alstory," Ekl and Sotos begin. "He represented Ciolino and Protess. On the same day he obtained the confession, Ciolino procured Rimland to defend Simon for free, thus ensuring that the confession and witness statements obtained by Northwestern would never be scrutinized."

The letter to Alvarez also takes a swipe at Devine's handling of the case. Without naming Devine, Sotos and Ekl assert that "the suppression of evidence exculpating [Simon] and inculpating

Porter is only partially attributable to Rimland's betrayal of his client. Unfortunately, a prior administration of the Cook County State's Attorney's office acquiesced in a coordinated effort between Northwestern representatives and a local media outlet to pressure the State's Attorney into a hasty and regrettable rush to judgment."

At Simon's sentencing, the letter continues, "ASA Gainer told the court that Senior and Beckwith, who gave inculpatory testimony against Porter, but said not a word about Alstory, would testify against Alstory. No one said a word about Edwards's testimony that he saw Porter shoot the victims. As a result, Alstory was misled to believe that if he went to trial, several witnesses, including the phony actor employed by Ciolino, would implicate him."

The letter also adds the following. "In 1999...Ciolino coerced [Simon's] false confession by convincing him Chicago police were on their way to arrest him, that they had sufficient evidence to put him on death row, and that by confessing to the murders in self-defense, he would serve a short prison stint and be rewarded with riches from book and movie deals upon release. Even the undisputed aspects of the interrogation are shocking and negate the integrity of the confession."

The two lawyers then discuss the contents of three affidavits from Inez's daughter Tiffany Jackson, Inez's sister Rita Carlisle, and the Reverend Braun, the Milwaukee community activist. Taken together, they shed additional light on the corrosion of the Simon case by Protess and Rimland.

Tiffany's affidavit stated that her mother had serious alcohol and drug problems and confirmed that Protess drove her and Inez to a Chicago hotel where large amounts of alcohol were provided to Inez. Tiffany also confirmed that Inez told her she was helping Porter because Protess would help free Walter and because Protess had promised her money from book rights.

In Rita's affidavit she said her sister Inez told her that Protess promised Inez money from book and movie deals, and that Abrams (the pro bono attorney Ciolino provided to Inez) told Inez in Rita's presence that she could to go jail if she did not stay true to her statement to Protess.

Reverend Braun stated he called Rimland and told him it was wrong for Alstory to plead guilty to a crime he did not commit. Rimland told Braun Alstory's innocence did not matter because he would get convicted at trial and get the death penalty.

Braun's affidavit states, "I also asked Rimland about the deal Simon told me he had with Ciolino and Protess, that if Simon plead guilty he would only do two years in jail. Rimland told me that Simon could trust Ciolino and Protess because they were both friends of his and that he did a lot of work with them. He even mentioned that he had worked with them to free Anthony Porter."

As far as Ekl and Sotos are concerned, it was not just the Simon case that had become woefully infected by Medill involvement. Their letter outlines a pattern in which they felt Protess had engaged in similar meddling in the local justice system to obtain his ends, which they considered nefarious.

On page seven of their letter, under the title, "2011–2012, Northwestern's Pattern of Coercing Witnesses Fully Emerges," they continue their allegations. The following is taken verbatim:

1. Ford Heights Four
   a. In his book, *A Promise of Justice,* Protess describes his efforts to convince key prosecution witness, Charles McCraney, to recant. Protess wrote that Ciolino dressed in a sharkskin suit and posed as Hollywood movie producer Jerry Bruckheimer for a meeting at a South Side KFC, at which Ciolino gave McCraney $80.00, showed him a movie contract, and promised McCraney money from a movie deal in exchange for his testimony.

b. In a separate handwritten note, Protess advised McCraney to contact him because Protess had "information for you that should be helpful financially."

c. McCraney has since told investigators that Protess told him he could "use" one of two female Northwestern students for a day or two if he recanted his earlier testimony.

2. People v. Madison Hobley[I]

a. The key prosecution witness, Andre Council, has testified Ciolino came to his home with Hobley's lawyer (Andrea Lyon, who was then teaching at DePaul University College of Law) and told him if he recanted, Ciolino would insure his daughter received a free education and that he would never have to work again.

3. People v. McKinney

a. At a minimum, CCSA prosecutors allege two witnesses were paid during student interviews. One witness recanted the statement he provided students. One witness told prosecutors the students were nice to him so he would "give them an interview...so they could get a good grade" and the female student had "come on to him," acting as if they were going to "give up some p+++y if I would talk to them."

b. Protess doctored an e-mail in an attempt to obstruct Northwestern University's efforts to determine whether he had waived a claimed reporter's privilege by disclosing documents to McKinney's lawyers.

4. People v. Serrano[II]

a. CCSA prosecutors allege a Northwestern memorandum demonstrates that "discussion of promises made to (a witness) is blatant and rampant" and student manipulation of that witness is abundant and apparent.

b. Prosecutors have unearthed e-mails in Serrano which claim Protess brought a female student to a meeting with a jailed witness as "a treat."

c. An email in Serrano shows Protess acknowledged an inherent conflict in asking his lawyer friend to represent a witness as a favor to him.

Ekl and Sotos also detail the wrongdoing that took place in the Simon case, which already has been enumerated. The attorneys close with this:

"Our client has been robbed of his freedom for 15 years as a result of Northwestern's unbridled fabrication of false evidence against him, the professional misconduct of a free lawyer who was supplied to Alstory by his own accusers, the failure of the CCSA's prior administration to stand up to Northwestern and the media by investigating the fabricated evidence against Alstory, and the refusal of the courts to take seriously the compelling evidence of Alstory's innocence and Porter's guilt. After all these years, justice requires that the shameful charade be exposed and concluded."

When asked for comment about the Sotos filing, Protess told the *Chicago Reader*, "Does Sotos seriously believe that my journalism students, a private investigator and a defense attorney actively collaborated with Cook County prosecutors and the Chief Judge to railroad an innocent man? Does that sound rational? Yeah, if you believe the Earth is flat or God created humans 5,000 years ago."

Those who believed that the day would never come when Alvarez would review the Simon case put forth a single explanation: Were such a review to become public, it would lead inevitably to troubling questions about how this terrible injustice was allowed to have happened and, more starkly, who was responsible for it.

Some of those troubling questions? How is it that Dick Devine, the State's Attorney in 1999 when this injustice took place, was unaware that one of his assistants, Tom Gainer, failed to fully disclose grand jury testimony to the sentencing judge? Was Devine unaware of the grand jury testimony inculpating Porter and exculpating Simon in the pool murders? Was he aware of that testimony and chose to ignore it? Did he ignore it because of all the bad press he was getting, that acknowledging that grand jury testimony would just add more fuel to the media fire?

How is it that John Lavine's oversight of his star professor was so loose that he was unaware of Protess's promising key witnesses money and sex with his female students in high-profile murder cases if, and only if, those key witnesses altered their testimony? (Additionally, Charles McCraney claimed that such a proposition was made during the Ford Heights Four case.)

How could Lavine remain ignorant of the fact that Protess and two of his female students left notes at McCraney's home, promising McCraney money, fame, and movie rights if he altered his testimony? After all, in his book, *Promise of Justice,* Protess spells out that episode in detail, describing how Ciolino told McCraney he was a Hollywood producer named Jerry Bruckheimer who would give movie rights to McCraney if he altered his Ford Heights Four testimony.

How was Lavine unaware that an armed Ciolino, who once threatened to shoot a south suburban man in the head and was fined $2,000 on another occasion for acting as a private eye when he was not licensed, was working behind the Medill scenes, "bullrushing" Simon into confessing, as Ciolino himself described it in a *Chicago Magazine* piece in July 2002—that while working with the Medill students, an armed Ciolino extracted an illegal confession from a Milwaukee man by using threats against his life, promises of riches, and lies about the length of time the confessing man would have to spend in jail?

Yet, despite bleak assumptions that Simon would never receive the hearing he deserved, in response to rising pressure Alvarez changed the long-held stance of the Cook County State's Attorney's office. Alvarez announced in late 2013 that she would review the Simon case, though she summarily dismissed calls by a subsequent *Chicago Tribune* editorial and a Zorn column that she appoint an independent prosecutor to undertake the review.

"No matter how objective her review team is or how overwhelming their conclusion might end up being, this case is such a tangled mess at this point that it demands the scrutiny of a special prosecutor whose independence is unquestioned," Zorn wrote.

In rebuffing the *Tribune,* Alvarez said that her office's Public Integrity Unit headed by Celeste Stack would undertake the review.

Discredited though Protess was, he wasted no time in setting up the Chicago Innocence Project (ChIP), located at 205 W. Monroe Street, in Chicago, in April 2011. ChIP was created as a not-for-profit with a mandate similar to Medill's Innocence Project. Namely, it would engage college students, community residents, private investigators, and journalists in reporting, exposing, and remedying mistakes made by the criminal justice system.

Initially, Protess was named President of ChIP. Pamela Cytrynbaum, a Chicago-based writer and teacher who covered criminal justice issues for the New Orleans *Times-Picayune,* was named executive director. Bethany Barratt, associate professor of political science at Roosevelt University and director of the Joseph Loundy Human Rights Initiative Project, an undergraduate cross-national human rights research program, was named faculty liaison.

Directors include Kenneth Adams, one of the Ford Heights Four defendants, and Dana Holland who was wrongfully arrested, convicted, and sentenced to 118 years in February 1993, for the armed robbery and attempted murder of Ella Wembley and the rape of Dionne Stanley.

On its home page, Protess explains the emergence of ChIP.

"Nonprofit investigative reporting groups are the wave of the future," he states. He then lists a number of similar non-profits that have cropped up in the recent past, dedicated to freeing the wrongfully convicted—ProPublica, the Better Government Association in Chicago, Center for Public Integrity, the Texas Tribune, the Voice of San Diego, and the Center for Investigative Reporting among them.[III]

Interestingly, among many other items the ChIP web site includes a copy of the entire forty-two-page transcript of the September 1999 Alstory Simon change of plea and sentencing hearing before Judge Fitzgerald. The transcript appears under the heading, "Related Documents in the Anthony Porter Case." From the standpoint of ChIP's mandate, posting this document is curious.[IV] The document serves as an outright embarrassment for the organization for, taken together with the February 1999 Gainer grand jury transcripts, it suggests Porter's guilt.

I   In the Hobley matter, a non-Innocence Project case, Madison Hobley was charged and convicted of burning down a three-story apartment building in 1987 in which seven people were killed, including his wife and his infant son. He later was exonerated and pardoned by then-Governor George Ryan. Hobley settled with the City of Chicago for $7 million.

II   Armando Serrano, an Innocence Project case, was convicted along with a codefendant of the 1993 slaying of a Humboldt Park resident as he left for work. The State's case rested on the testimony of a jailhouse snitch who claimed the men confessed to him and the victim's widow who offered a possible motive for the crime. A decade later, the snitch admitted he had lied, and the widow recanted.

III   Beneath the title, "Watchdogs over the Justice System," the home page also reveals the ChIP wrongful conviction project of the moment. That is the case of Armando Serrano noted by Ekl and Sotos in their letter to State's Attorney Alvarez. Serrano was accused along with another man, Jose Mantanez, of gunning down Rodrigo Vargas during an armed robbery as Rodrigo was leaving for work in the Humboldt Park neighborhood in 1993. Wilda Vargas, the victim's widow, testified at Serrano's trial along with a jailhouse snitch, which led to the convictions of the two men. Both were sentenced to fifty-five years for murder.

Protess and his students had worked the Serrano case while he was still at the Innocence Project in Evanston, but when he was let go by Northwestern in spring 2011, he brought the Serrano case with him to ChIP. There is something of a pattern in the wrongful-conviction cases Protess pursues, and Serrano fits that pattern.

- The case is over two decades old. This resembles the Porter case, which was seventeen years old; the McKinney case, which was twenty-five years old; and the Ford Heights Four case, which was nearly two decades old.
- The case is laced with recantations that were made years later by key witnesses. Again, this is similar to the Porter, McKinney, and Ford Heights Four cases.
- And also like the three predecessor cases, the Serrano case is polluted by the unprofessional involvement of Medill students possessing few life experiences who are pushing their investigative techniques to the ethical limit.

For example, after meeting with a group of Medill students in her home in 2006, Wilda Vargas signed an affidavit attesting that she harbored nagging doubts about whether a gas station altercation between her late husband and the defendants had led to her husband's murder after all. And now she wants to set the record straight by testifying at a court hearing that will determine whether Serrano and Mantanez win new trials. This is again similar to the affidavits signed in the Ford Heights Four case, the Porter case, and the McKinney case.

And there is the sworn affidavit of the jailhouse snitch who provided key testimony at the 1993 trial. Just like the Ford Heights Four case, the jailhouse snitch, a stick-up man who got a sweet deal in exchange for testifying in the case, also recanted his trial testimony years later in a signed affidavit. It is on the basis of the recantations and similar issues that ChIP and Serrano's lawyers are now petitioning for a new trial.

IV   Protess's former student Shawn Armbrust is also included as the Executive Director of the Mid-Atlantic Innocence Project. After Medill, Armbrust graduated cum laude from the Georgetown University Law Center. She includes a testimonial on the ChIP web site in which, without irony, she attributes her career success to her participation in obtaining freedom for Anthony Porter: "I was lucky. I chose to work on the Porter case, which ended in exoneration. I can't really describe how many doors that opened for me. Doing both the investigation and the media interviews that followed gave me a confidence and poise at a young age that I never would have been able to obtain otherwise."

15

The Alstory Simon
Indictment / Porter Freed

Of all the unanswered questions weaving through Alstory Simon's bizarre and frightful passage through the Cook County justice system, the greatest of them all is perhaps this: Why were
three grand juries convened in 1999 before Alstory Simon was
indicted for the pool murders? The answer to that question remains a genuine mystery.

First was the grand jury that was convened by Cook County
Assistant State's Attorney Thomas Gainer in February 1999 and
bears the identification GJ#363. That was the grand jury that
heard testimony from eleven witnesses—five men who were at
the pool the night of the murders and six members of the Medill
team. As has been seen, the February grand jury achieved three
ends: One, it again implicated Porter in the pool shootings; two, it
proved Simon was innocent of those murders; and three, it made
a mockery of Medill's so-called investigation. However, in the end,
that grand jury was dissolved without returning an indictment.

There was apparently a second grand jury convened by Gainer
on March 2, 1999, and bears the identification SGJ#2410, as in
"special grand jury number 2410." At least one witness appeared
before those proceedings—Carl Morrow, who was also at the pool
at the time of the shootings.

Morrow's testimony is favorable to Porter, and is the only sworn grand jury testimony uttered anywhere in this record that puts Alstory Simon and Inez at the pool. Under questioning by Gainer, Morrow says that he was a friend of Porter and of several members of Porter's family. He also testified that he saw Alstory Simon, Inez, and the two victims sitting in the upper bleachers and that he spotted Alstory and Inez fleeing the pool after the shootings. Additionally Morrow testified that while Porter also was at the pool—a fact that Porter has forever denied—he was so far away, at the southern end of the bleachers, that he could not have possibly killed the two victims. Who else, if anybody, was called to testify before the special grand jury is not known. What is known is that this grand jury, like the first, returned no indictment.

And a third grand jury was convened by Gainer on March 25, 1999, identification GJ#407. That grand jury, which sat for only a couple of hours before it indicted Simon, heard from only two witnesses, neither of whom had any direct knowledge of the pool murders. The two witnesses were a Chicago Police Department detective named Allen Szudarski and Celeste Stack.

Again, Celeste Stack is the assistant state's attorney in charge of the Conviction Integrity Unit who, if anyone, was expected to provide a valuable role in Ekl's and Sotos's efforts to get a hearing for Simon. The same Celeste Stack who, two days after Christmas 2005, questioned Inez Jackson at length and heard the dying woman declare time and again that her ex-husband Alstory was innocent, and that she had lied about Alstory's involvement in the murders because Protess had offered her money and help in getting her son and nephew out of prison. The same Cook County ASA who came away unpersuaded from that dreary Inez encounter concluding that she, Stack, did not find Inez's testimony compelling. Certainly not compelling enough to warrant a post-conviction hearing for Simon.

Questions about the third grand jury abound. When Stack appeared before the grand jury on March 25, 1999, and gave testimony that led to Simon's indictment, was she aware of the testimony generated by Gainer during the February grand jury? Did Gainer tell her about that grand jury testimony exculpating Simon? And if he did, did Stack gratuitously offer that testimony to the third grand jury so that jurors could more judiciously decide whether or not to return an indictment against Simon? Or was that grand jury asked by Gainer to vote a true bill against Simon even though he and possibly Stack knew that no meaningful grand jury evidence of any kind existed to indict Simon?[1]

The larger question is this. How and why is it that Gainer allowed an indictment to be returned against Simon in late March when that same prosecutor spent endless hours in February 1999 listening to five pool witnesses testify, one after the other, that Porter was the killer? Why were these witnesses not called before the March 25 grand jury?

Had Gainer forgotten the exchange with Kenneth Edwards from February 1999, as he questioned secondhand witnesses Stack and Szudarski on March 25, an exchange that took place seventeen years after the pool murders?

GAINER: As you sit here today, can you tell this grand jury who it was who fired those shots?

EDWARDS: I sure can.

GAINER: Who was it?

EDWARDS: It was Tony Porter.

GAINER: And the people that you saw coming down the stairs calmly before the woman started to stagger, do you know who either of those two people were?

EDWARDS: One was Tony Porter. The other guy I did not know.

And how about the February grand juror puzzling with Edwards over Simon's confession?

JUROR: Now that you have seen pictures of Alstory Simon in the newspaper, could that other person have been Alstory Simon?

EDWARDS: No, it could not have been.

JUROR: Why would Simon say he did it now and he didn't say it then?

EDWARDS: Your guess is as good as mine. It just makes me laugh that the situation is the way it is now.

And what was Detective Allen Szudarski doing before this grand jury? Why did Gainer not call Charles Salvatore and Dennis Gray? After all, they were the Area One Violent Crime detectives who originally investigated the case in 1982. They were the investigators who interviewed the pool witnesses, took statements from them, and took them through police mug-shot books and lineups at Area One. They also, it is remembered, were the detectives who beat back Montgomery's and Porter's attempt to win a $25 million judgment against the two detectives and the City for allegedly mishandling the investigation.

Detective Szudarski had no prior involvement in the Porter/ Simon investigation. The information he had about the case was what he read in reports generated by Salvatore and Gray and the various affidavits that initially fingered Simon before they were all recanted. While he surely read the Salvatore and Gray reports, he must have withheld them from the grand jury because those reports reflect an open-and-shut case against Porter.

A possible explanation for this peculiar grand jury is, of course, that Devine and Gainer, possibly at Devine's direction, sought a surefire indictment. To this end they could consciously choose to avoid witnesses that could contradict that objective, like the pool witnesses. They might choose instead to call Celeste Stack, whose career is in the state's attorney's office and who was unpersuaded by Inez's testimony recanting her accusations against Alstory Simon, and a detective whose knowledge of the case could come only from old reports. If the state's attorney and the detective are given reports that implicate Simon, then their testimony will be informed only by damning evidence—Inez's confession, Alstory Simon's own confession, and the record of Alstory apologizing to Marilyn Green's mother and children in open court. They would also have reviewed affidavits that directly stated Simon's guilt without knowing that the affidavits were signed in the belief that there was a quid pro quo with David Protess, that they would have their long prison sentences reduced, or that they would receive money, or both.

Neither Gainer nor Stack nor even Devine has shown any interest in clearing up this confusion. In fact, in a January 2, 2015, op-ed piece in the *Chicago Tribune* authored by Devine and titled "We followed the evidence," the former state's attorney attempts to put a reasonable face on this grave miscarriage of justice that took place on his watch. He fails utterly to achieve his goal.

In reality, his op-ed piece is filled with banal generalities and misrepresentations of key facts. For openers, Devine writes that a grand jury was convened to review the case and heard evidence "not only pointing toward Simon but also evidence implicating Porter. After reviewing the evidence, the grand jury indicted Simon for the murders."

To which grand jury is Devine referring? While that representation may be true with regard to the March 25 grand jury—though it is unlikely, since that grand jury returned a Simon indictment in a couple of hours—it is certainly a mischaracterization of the February 1999 grand jury. As has been noted several times, the February 1999 grand jury heard five witnesses, all of whom had been at the pool the night of the 1982 murders and all of whom named Porter as the killer. Moreover, it was a grand jury session in which Gainer blew holes through the integrity of the Innocence Project investigation.

A second absurdity is Devine's claim that Gainer knew Rimland "as an experienced defense attorney hardly considered a push-over." The fact is, Rimland had received the grand jury materials generated by Gainer just seven months before Simon's sentencing—from Gainer. Yet he never breathed a word to the sentencing judge that his client had not once been mentioned by witnesses as having been at the pool, let alone being responsible for the shootings. As we have seen, Rimland never challenged the illegal and outrageous confession extracted from his client by his West Jackson Boulevard officemate. And he misrepresented and fabricated other evidence during sentencing, as has been seen. This hardly-considered-a-pushover lawyer seems to have abandoned legal ethics when it came to representing Alstory Simon.

Yet another Devine mischaracterization appears deep in the op-ed piece in which he writes, "The reality is that prosecutors were presented with evidence that someone other than Porter was responsible for the Washington Park murders." Where, one might ask, where is the evidence in the February grand jury that someone other than Porter was responsible? The answer is *nowhere*.

Perhaps Devine was referring to the confession extracted by Ciolino. If so, the confession was illegal and would have been tossed out upon challenge by Rimland, and the former state's attorney surely knew that. Maybe Devine is referring to the statements against Simon by Inez.

A final point. Devine makes much of the fact that "Simon gave a videotaped statement to Paul Ciolino, a private investigator working with Northwestern University's Medill Innocence Project, confessing" to the murders. He goes on to say that prosecutors obtained a copy of that video and studied it closely. Yet as Epach notes in his affidavit, no one ever called in Ciolino to determine the facts surrounding the confession. Was it forced? Was it obtained at gunpoint? Did Ciolino tell Simon that accidents happen every day, even in one's own home, and that an accident could happen to Simon that very morning if he did not confess to the murders? Did Ciolino "bull rush" Simon in such a way that Simon "could not recover," as Ciolino told *Chicago Magazine* in 2002? Ciolino was never questioned. Instead veteran prosecutors in Devine's office, according to Devine, obtained a copy of the taped confession and sat around watching it, judging the merits of the confession based on a viewing of a dubbed videotape.

I   These transcripts never became part of the case, so they are not public.

16

A Taste
of Freedom

By late 2014, Alvarez, Stack, and her colleagues in the Conviction Integrity Unit had viewed the completed ninety-three-minute *Death in the Park* documentary by Shawn Rech not once but twice at Alvarez's request. The film, coproduced by Rech and Andrew Hale, a Chicago attorney, and directed by Brandon Kimber, a Rech assistant, by then had had a premier screening before a large audience in Chicago and soon would be unveiled at DOC NYC, a prestigious invitation-only, documentary film festival in New York City.

By the end of October 2014, Alvarez and her top assistants had called in more than one hundred individuals for questioning about the case over a nearly year-long period. And Alvarez had come to an irrevocable conclusion: Alstory Simon must be freed. To that end, Alvarez appeared before Chief Criminal Court Judge Paul Biebel, Jr. at 9 A.M. on October 30 and requested that the conviction of Simon be vacated and that he be released immediately, requests that Judge Biebel immediately granted. Interesting questions remained, however—how would Alvarez frame the release? Who would take the fall for it?

Only minutes after Biebel granted the request that morning, Alvarez strode into an upper-floor conference room in the Leighton Criminal Courts building. The room was packed wall-to-wall with camera crews, reporters, and various interested onlookers, including Marty Preib and me.

As we awaited Alvarez's announcement, there was not another reporter in that room who had an inkling about the specifics of Gainer's duplicity, Rimland's mind-boggling "representation" of Simon, Protess's offers of money to Inez, or Epach's or Monahan's affidavits. Nor did they know the details of how Ciolino extracted his illegal confession. Nor did they have a clue about Earl Lewis getting shot in the head by Porter for Lewis's objections to Porter kicking his dog or Douglas McGhee's getting beaten to a pulp by Porter in the pool bleachers under a hot summer sun before Porter robbed McGhee of $800. Nor did they have a clue as to Porter's 1983 trial alibi put in by Fat Luke. None of the other reporters had spent even a few minutes educating himself or herself about the long background of the Porter/Simon saga.

As silence fell over the room, Alvarez began by noting that the murder and voluntary manslaughter charges against Simon had been vacated at her office's request by Biebel at 9 A.M. that day. She then engaged in a brief history of the pool shootings, Porter's conviction and sentencing, and Simon's subsequent confession and his sentencing.

"This case has undoubtedly been the most complicated and most challenging reinvestigation that we have undertaken, but justice compels that I take action today," she began. "At the end of the day and in the best interest of justice, we could reach no other conclusion but that the investigation of this case has been so deeply corroded and corrupted that we can no longer maintain the legitimacy of this conviction," she added.

Alvarez then heaped boundless blame for the wrongful incarceration on Protess, Ciolino, and Rimland. She questioned the integrity of Protess and criticized the private investigator Ciolino, who obtained Simon's videotaped confession using an actor to falsely implicate Simon, saying that his tactics were "coercive" and "unacceptable by law enforcement standards." She also raised questions of the independence of attorney Jack Rimland, who agreed to represent Simon at the suggestion of Ciolino, whom Rimland knew.

"The bottom line," Alvarez said, "is the investigation conducted by Protess and private investigator Ciolino as well as the subsequent legal representation of Mr. Simon [was] so flawed that it's clear the constitutional rights of Mr. Simon were not scrupulously protected as our law requires." She then indicated that she would have considered obstruction of justice or witness intimidation charges if the statute of limitations hadn't run out. "In my twenty-eight years as a prosecutor, I've never seen a detective take a confession from someone and then say, 'Hey, and then I got a lawyer for you,'" she told reporters. "This relationship raises very serious questions about a legal conflict of interest."

Protess, now President of ChiP, had been widely visible when Porter was freed, posing for exultant photographs and answering reporters' questions. On October 30 he was nowhere to be found, nor did he issue any kind of statement.

Warden, however, now the executive director emeritus of the Center on Wrongful Convictions, offered his own brief analysis of the Simon case. "I have studied hundreds of false confessions. Alstory Simon's fits no known pattern. Usually, false confessions are promptly recanted.... Not only was Alstory's not promptly recanted, but months later he pleaded guilty in open court and apologized to the victims' families."

Ciolino also issued a statement, which by October 30, 2014, sounded like a broken record, again misrepresenting the facts of the case. Among other things, he says that he, Protess, and the Medill students saved Porter from execution, which is a questionable idea at best. "I believe Anthony Porter was innocent, but no one can deny the State fell far short of meeting the standard of beyond a reasonable doubt in securing a death sentence for him,"

Ciolino wrote. "But for the work we did together with David Protess and his students, Porter's life would have been taken." For this last statement to be true, one must assume that had they failed to frame Simon for murders for which Porter had been convicted, Porter would eventually have been executed, irrespective of the never-completed competency hearing or anything else. For it to be the truth, Governor Ryan had only one reason for placing a moratorium on the death penalty in Illinois—Anthony Porter's innocence, as demonstrated by Ciolino, Protess, and a fungible cast of Medill students. (In reality, Governor Ryan's moratorium was prompted by the Porter case, but it was not the sole reason for the governor's actions. He went on to issue a blanket clemency for the prisoners awaiting execution in Illinois on January 3, 2003. On March 9, 2011, Governor Pat Quinn abolished the death penalty in Illinois.)

Around noon on October 30, 2014, nearly fifteen years after he had been promised by former Medill Professor David Protess that he would do only two years in prison and would reap a fortune when he got out after serving those two years, Alstory Simon approached the entranceway of the Illinois Department of Corrections prison in Jacksonville, a few miles west of the state capital. He signed a couple of documents, handed them to a prison guard, and, toting a cardboard box containing all of his earthly belongings, stepped into the daylight of freedom. A misting rain fell from gray autumn skies. Clad in jeans, a pair of new construction boots, and a hoodie, he walked to a nearby black Mercedes sport utility vehicle driven by Sean Rech, the Cleveland filmmaker. Fighting back tears, Simon talked about how he had missed the death of his mother while locked up.

"I'm not angry at the system, I'm angry at the people that did what they did to me," he said, before closing the passenger-side window. He was penniless.

17

A Life Resumes

With Alstory Simon sitting in the passenger seat and two members of his camera crew in the rear, Rech pulled away from the prison walls and the towering guardhouses. He exited the cyclone-fence-enclosed parking lot and headed back to Chicago, where Simon had lived until 1982 when he, his wife Inez, and Inez's four kids moved to Milwaukee to free themselves from the gang violence, moral corruption, and social chaos that coursed through daily life in the Chicago Housing Authority's Robert Taylor Homes where they had lived for several years.

As the black Mercedes drove through Jacksonville and across U.S. Interstate 72 and up I-55 to its destination more than 200 miles to the north, Simon was under no illusions about the challenges that lay before him. Thanksgiving was little more than three weeks off, and there would be the emotional and psychological challenges associated with reconnecting with close members of his large, extended family, most of whom he had not seen or talked with in years.

At age sixty-four, Simon faced myriad visits to the doctor. A variety of lab tests and physical examinations would be an essential part of that road to make up for the substandard medical care that attended his decade-and-a-half incarceration. It would be only a day or two before Simon would discover one of the great physical challenges of freedom following his years of incarceration: climbing into a real bed with clean sheets, a real pillow, and a firm mattress and trying to get a sound night's sleep amid peace and quiet, which at first proved almost impossible. No prison guards checked on him several times during the nighttime hours, banging on iron bars with beaming flashlights amid the echoing background noise of hundreds and hundreds of other inmates. Long before, the nocturnal prison disturbances had become the new normal for the imprisoned Simon, over time providing him with a strange and surreal lullaby, almost. Now, trying to sleep like a normal, free person was a very real challenge he had to overcome.

There were some upsides for Simon, small though they were, considering what he had endured. On the evening of October 30, 2014, the day of his release, he ate a celebratory dinner at Gibson's Steak House in Rosemont. With glad-handing members of the ad hoc group in attendance—attorneys Jim Sotos and Andrew Hale, Rech and members of his film crew, former federal agents Jimmy Delorto and Johnny Mazzola, and me, among others—Simon dove into a prime T-bone steak for the first time in his life with a glass of whiskey for the first time in fifteen years. He ate in virtual stunned silence.

There also was the real likelihood that he would soon be granted a certificate of innocence, which Ekl and Sotos were seeking from a Cook County Criminal Court Judge. Once granted, the certificate of innocence would entitle Simon to a one-time payout of more than $200,000 from the Illinois Court of Claims for his wrongful incarceration.

For Rech and Hale, their documentary *Murder in the Park* had already been screened in Chicago, Cleveland, and New York and was drawing increased interest from several investors wanting to bankroll an effort to take the documentary to big screens nationwide and/or to cable TV.

For Jimmy and Johnny of Delorto Mazzola Associates of Batavia, the one-time ATF agents who had spotted Simon's televised confession and immediately realized that it was a "crock of shit," and without whom the Alstory Simon story might never have surfaced publicly, it was back to the grind—driving through the Land of Lincoln's outback and Chicago's inner city and suburbs, serving subpoenas and obtaining sworn affidavits from would-be witnesses in other civil cases on behalf of Ekl, Sotos, and other Illinois attorneys.

For me, the author of this book and the report "Chimera," the next step was a recasting of that first take on the Alstory Simon injustice in the form of this bound book from Amika Press of Chicago—a recasting with a new title, *Justice Perverted: How the Innocence Project at Northwestern University's Medill School of Journalism Sent an Innocent Man to Prison.*

It bears repeating that *Justice Perverted* is grounded almost exclusively in the sworn testimony underlying thousands of pages of the public record, with virtually no first-person interviews included. That is simply because few of the key players in this woeful tale will talk about it.

In closing out this decade-and-a-half-long upending of justice in the Cook County Court system, there is a stark and inescapable conclusion that must be noted. For this perversion of justice to have succeeded from the outset and to have gone on for as long as it did, members of the media and four specific individuals had to abandon their professional obligations. Assistant State's Attorney Tom Gainer, Simon's lawyer Jack Rimland, investigator Paul Ciolino, and Northwestern Professor David Protess all had to ignore or fail in their presumed roles in order for Simon to replace Porter in prison.

Had the media taken the time to examine the sworn underlying record, they would have discovered at once that Porter, not Simon, was in fact the 1982 Washington Park pool triggerman.

Had Gainer told Thomas Fitzgerald, the sentencing judge, about the February 1999 grand jury inquiry that reinforced Porter's 1983 conviction and exculpated Simon, the judge would have called a halt to the proceedings.

Had Rimland revealed to Judge Fitzgerald how the phony confession had been extracted from his client by Ciolino or that he rented office space from Ciolino or that he was representing Simon thanks to a referral from Ciolino and was taking the case for free, again the sentencing hearing would have come to a halt.

Had Ciolino acted in concert with his profession's ethical guidelines, instead of threatening Simon with physical harm and "bull-rushing" him until he "just could not recover," there never would have been a phony and illegal confession in the first place.

And, of course, had Professor David Protess's agenda been confined to training investigative journalists, his students would have sought the truth of Porter's situation instead of searching for evidence in support of a pre-conclusion. Had those students been chasing the truth, it seems unlikely they would have ignored so much evidence that incriminated Porter, and it seems even more unlikely that they would have convinced themselves that Simon was guilty of the crime for which Porter had been convicted.

All it would have taken was for one of these players in this tragic miscarriage of justice to have acted professionally and with good conscience, and Simon never would have been sentenced to thirty-seven years in prison for a crime he did not commit.

Epilogue:
Payback Time

On February 17, 2015, three attorneys representing Alstory Si-mon—Terry Ekl, Jim Sotos, and Andrew Hale—marched into the Dirksen Federal building at 219 S. Dearborn Street in Chicago and filed a federal lawsuit with the District Court Clerk on the twentieth floor. Named as defendants in the lawsuit were North-western University; David Protess, the former Medill journalism professor of twenty-nine years; Paul J. Ciolino, the private inves-tigator; and Jack P. Rimland, Simon's former attorney.

The nine-count complaint seeks more than $40 million in pu-nitive damages from the four defendants for conspiring to effect Simon's wrongful conviction and incarceration. The lawsuit ac-cuses the defendants of malicious prosecution, failure of the uni-versity to properly supervise Protess and Ciolino in their zeal to "free prisoners who were allegedly wrongfully convicted," negli-gence by the University in its supervision of Protess and Cioli-no, and conspiracy among all four defendants along with other charges of wrongdoing.

The fifty-page complaint filed by Simon's attorneys is sweep-ing in scope, beginning with "The Rise of David Protess" in 1981 when he joined the Medill faculty, and tracing a path through the Dowaliby case; the Ford Heights Four case; and the Armando

Serrano, Anthony McKinney, and the Alstory Simon cases. The lawsuit then turns to "The Fall of David Protess," with a detailed account of how Protess's underhanded involvement in the Serrano and McKinney cases led to his suspension and firing by the university in the spring of 2011.

The lawsuit begins with a simple truth.

"In 1999, plaintiff Alstory Simon was wrongfully incarcerated for a double murder he did not commit. Arrested at the age of forty-eight, Simon spent more than fifteen years in prison before he was ultimately exonerated on October 30, 2014" by a Cook County judge at the request of State's Attorney Anita Alvarez.

It then turns to the heart of the complaint.

"The horrific injustice that befell Simon occurred when Defendants, Northwestern University, Professor David Protess, private investigator Paul Ciolino, and attorney Jack Rimland conspired to frame Simon for the murders in order to secure the release of the real killer, Anthony Porter."

The complaint continues:

"As part of a Northwestern University Investigative Journalism class he taught in 1998, Protess instructed his students to investigate Porter's case and develop evidence of Porter's innocence, rather than to search for the truth. During that investigation, Northwestern, through its employees and/or agents, Protess and Ciolino, intentionally manufactured false witness statements against Simon and then used the fabricated evidence, along with terrifying threats and other illegal and deceitful tactics to coerce a knowingly false confession from Simon."

As part of the conspiracy, the lawsuit contends, Protess and Ciolino hired "Jack Rimland to represent Simon. Acting in concert with Protess and Ciolino, Rimland coerced Simon to plead guilty despite his innocence by lying to Simon about the strength of the evidence against him, withholding compelling eyewitness grand jury testimony implicating Porter and threatening Simon."

As for Protess's class, the suit alleges, it was not a journalism class at all as the students during the entire fall 1998 semester did not "create or submit any articles for review or publication." Instead, the suit asserts, the students were used as "pawns to deflect public scrutiny from the blatantly illegal and unethical investigative techniques routinely employed by Northwestern's employees and/or agents to generate statements from witnesses without regard to the truth or falsity of those statements."

According to the lawsuit, Protess's ascendancy to journalism stardom began with his and Rob Warden's 1990 investigation of David Dowaliby, who had been convicted in 1990 of murdering his seven-year-old adopted daughter. The subsequent publication of *Gone in the Night,* a book about the Dowaliby case by Protess and Warden, along with a 1996 airing by CBS of a two-part series based on the Dowaliby case, "enhanced the reputation, prestige, and popularity of Northwestern and its Medill School of Journalism," the lawsuit alleged.

"After the Dowaliby case," the suit claims, "Northwestern converted the Medill Investigative Journalism class into a vehicle to manufacture cases establishing innocence in order to exonerate allegedly wrongfully convicted individuals."

The lawsuit then analyzes Protess's involvement in the Ford Heights Four case and mentions a book written by Protess and Warden about that case, *A Promise of Justice.* This section of the suit reprises the underhanded dealings that attended the Ford Heights Four Case. These include:

- Protess's March 14, 1996, letter to Charles McCraney in which he advises McCraney he has "monetary rights" to his story, but only if he described "his observations consistently with Northwestern's view" of the case

- Protess's March 13, 1996, note to McCraney, which he left on Mc-Craney's front door advising him to contact Protess as Protess had something that "should be helpful <u>financially</u>" (underscore Protess) to McCraney

- Protess and Ciolino's meeting with McCraney in a Kankakee KFC restaurant in which Ciolino falsely portrayed himself as Hollywood producer Jerry Bruckheimer and told McCraney that he, McCraney, stood to make a small fortune in return for his changed testimony

- Protess's, Ciolino's, and Northwestern Medill students' repeated attempts "to get the eyewitness to change his testimony with Protess offering him $250,000 and 20 percent in 'upfront' money for his rights" in a book and movie deal

- Protess's offer to the eyewitness that he "could have sex with either of two Northwestern Medill students if he would change his testimony"

The lawsuit also refers to a passage in Protess's *A Promise of Justice* in which Ira Johnson, ultimately convicted for his involvement in the killings of Carol Schmal and Larry Lionberg, had written a follow-up letter to Stacy Delo, a Protess student working on the Ford Heights Four case who had paid him a visit in prison.

The letter, in an envelope with the letters "SWAK" scrawled across the back—as in "sealed with a kiss"—begins, "Hello beautiful." After wishing her well, Johnson got right to the point.

"I really had a nice time with you and Laura [Sullivan] and I did have things to talk about.... Maybe you will get the opportunity to hear what you been wanting (sic) to hear.... I couldn't get you off my mind, all I could think about was your bedroom eyes—they are very, very, very sexy looking...Stacey, (sic) you are one sexy-ass woman to be a white girl."

If Stacy would return for another visit, the suit alleges, Johnson promised, "It will be well worth your time."

Quoting *A Promise of Justice*, the suit alleges that Ciolino taught the Medill students a "Ghetto 101" class to prepare young Caucasians from upscale backgrounds how to conduct interviews in downscale neighborhoods. "Go [for interviews] before the gang-bangers wake up and wear running shoes," Ciolino cautioned his students, the suit alleges. He also taught them the art of questioning witnesses through a so-called "good cop, bad cop" routine.

The suit alleges that in the wake of the Ford Heights Four case, certain ranking members of the Medill faculty were becoming suspicious of Protess's teaching methods, yet they turned a blind eye because of the fame and fortune his persona was bringing to Medill.

"Northwestern knowingly approved, encouraged, and ratified Protess's and Ciolino's deceitful and unethical conduct because Northwestern wanted to continue to reap the benefits, both in terms of prestige and financial gains, from Protess, Ciolino, and the students exposing alleged wrongful convictions."

In 1997 Michael Janeway, dean of the Medill School of Journalism, announced that after six years as head of Medill he was stepping down. He was returning to teaching at Columbia University, a school he admired in a city he and his wife loved, and where he had close friends on the faculty. Before his announcement, however, the suit claims he had "expressed concerns to Northwestern over the lack of oversight and supervision of Protess and Ciolino and a desire to cancel Protess's Investigative Journalism classes."

Yet, rather than act on Janeway's "valid and alarming concerns," the university, in conscious disregard of the consequences of Protess's and Ciolino's conduct and misuse of the Medill classes and students, replaced Dean Janeway with Ken Bode, a dean who "would support and/or ignore Protess's and Ciolino's unethical, deceitful, and/or illegal conduct."

The lawsuit references a May 23, 2000, *Daily Northwestern* article that described Bode as keeping Protess from leaving Northwestern and quoted Bode as helping to "keep David Protess in business." Moreover, in September 1998, Dean Bode moderated a Northwestern panel discussion of the Ford Heights Four case.

"Through all of this activity, again, Northwestern became aware of Protess's and Ciolino's deceitful and unethical investigatory techniques, but rather than putting an end to these techniques, encouraged Protess to continue to employ those techniques in the hopes that Protess would continue" to exonerate allegedly wrongfully convicted individuals and continue to heap "praise, recognition, and monetary benefits upon the University."

The suit then notes that in August 1998, the Robert R. McCormick Tribune Foundation made a $20 million grant to the Medill School of Journalism. In reality, to the extent that it matters, Northwestern/Medill's Innocence Project was fairly well funded. For example, in the 1990s the Alphawood Foundation, which had been established by Chicago radio-station mogul Fred Eychaner, regularly donated between $100,000 and $200,000 a year. The cash was essentially at the disposal of David Protess.

In that section of the lawsuit titled "The Fall of David Protess," the lawsuit enumerates fifteen separate instances in which Protess and his then-students engaged in wide-ranging "manipulation, trickery, and misleading information" to further their objectives of freeing McKinney and Serrano, both of whom were serving long prison sentences for murder. Four examples spelled out in the lawsuit will suffice.

- In 2004, a Medill student advised a Northwestern attorney that the Innocence Project team intended to bring a female Medill student to a state prison as a "treat" for a key witness whose statement they were attempting to obtain in the Serrano case.
- In 2004, a Northwestern employee and/or agent gave a key witness in the McKinney case $40 to buy crack cocaine in return for his

statement (which the witness later recanted) and attempted to disguise the payment by using an unknowing cab driver to pay the witness.

- In 2004, an incarcerated witness in the Serrano case stated that he provided the Medill team with a statement in the case (which he later recanted and acknowledged was false), solely because several female Medill students visited him and flirted with and flattered him. The witness stated that the female students sent him cards and letters when he was released from prison.
- In 2010, a Medill student writing about her experiences in an article titled "A Bad-Ass P.I. Spices Up the Quest for Truth," described a Northwestern investigator having her hide his loaded semiautomatic pistol in her purse as part of a practical joke about a pretend armed robbery.

The suit devoted fifteen pages to reprising the Simon debacle, which already has been examined closely in this book. Beginning with Simon's 1999 videotaped confession, it follows the sorry path through the various affidavits that were later recanted, the Gainer February 1999 grand jury testimony, and the array of mistruths uttered by Rimland during the sentencing of Simon. It also quotes the lengthy 2011 statement the university issued explaining why it was severing Protess from Northwestern's payroll and the decision by Alvarez to vacate Simon's conviction and free him on October 30, 2014.

The suit wraps up with the following: Alstory Simon was imprisoned for more than fifteen of his "most productive years and now, at the age of sixty-four, he must attempt to reconstruct a life for himself from scratch. Plaintiff was stripped without warning of all of his personal relationships, belongings, goals, and aspirations, and during the ensuing fifteen years, he was deprived of all of life's basic pleasures and offerings.

"During that time, plaintiff lost his mother, was unable to attend her funeral, and was unable to experience any joy or share life's joys with friends, family, and acquaintances."

The complaint concludes, Alstory Simon "respectfully requests that this court enter judgment in his favor and against defendants Northwestern University, David Protess, Paul J. Ciolino, and Jack P. Rimland, jointly and severally, for compensatory damages in a sum in excess of $40 million, punitive damages, costs as well as any other relief the court deems just and appropriate."

Though there is no way of knowing for certain what will happen, it seems probable that while Northwestern might contest the lawsuit initially, ultimately it will settle the case out of court, for a high price, thus avoiding the public relations' nightmare the university would otherwise be facing.

It seems unimaginable that Northwestern University will stand by to watch Protess take the witness stand, be sworn in, and face questions before a federal jury, with the media looking on from the courtroom gallery. The questions are disturbingly easy to predict. Had he ever promised key witnesses in criminal cases that they could have sex with his female students if they changed their testimony to accord with the former professor's agenda? Did he ever tell witnesses that they would reap huge fortunes through movie and book deals or that their prison sentences would be reduced or eliminated entirely, but only if those witnesses changed their testimony? And so on.

There would be additional witnesses tied to the university that would be called to testify if the suit reached a federal courtroom. The Ekl/Sotos complaint centers, in the main, on charges that the university was negligent in providing oversight and supervision of Protess. Certainly, therefore, high on the plaintiff's witness list would be former Dean John Lavine, and possibly even Lavine's predecessor, Ken Bode.

Even if Northwestern avoided airing all of the dirty laundry in a federal court, its reputation was in some jeopardy. For example, Rech's documentary *Murder in the Park* had already been screened in Chicago, Cleveland, and New York, and was drawing increased interest from several investors wanting to bankroll an effort to take the documentary to big screens nationwide and/ or to cable TV.

By all indications, additional similar lawsuits would follow completion of the Northwestern litigation—lawsuits against certain other individuals who served under Devine and had a role in the wrongdoing.

As of June 2015, the suit had not been settled.

Afterword:
"Chimera's" Aftermath

Until around 2009 or 2010, Alstory Simon's saga languished pretty much in limbo, but for periodic sorties by Jimmy Delorto and Johnny Mazzola into the Illinois outback or Chicago's inner city to chase down yet another fruitless lead or a trip to visit the imprisoned Simon in Danville. The campaign to get the prisoner a hearing gradually began to take on a new head of steam in early 2010, however, with the Internet publication of "Chimera," as mentioned at the outset of this book.

As noted, "Chimera" was sent to hundreds of people, including many members of the media. In 2010, the press was generally hostile or indifferent to the Alstory Simon case. Perhaps the idea that a professor at such a venerated journalism school had, with help from an unscrupulous private investigator, actually framed an innocent man was an unthinkable concept. Whatever the reason, local media paid little attention to the approximately 100-page report.

This lack of interest in examining the underlying facts of the case reached the very top of the local news organizations. At my request, the *Tribune* editorial board agreed to meet with Ekl and Sotos in mid-summer 2010 to hear a Sotos presentation of the Simon case. I hoped to get a favorable editorial out of the meeting.

Bruce Dold, editor of the editorial page, had gathered eight fellow board members. The Sotos presentation consumed an hour and a half, a practically unheard-of duration, stirring hopes among Ekl, Sotos, and me that a favorable editorial was at hand.

One member of the board had been assigned to read "Chimera" in preparation of the board meeting. He opened the gathering with the question, "Do you have any new evidence?" If he had read the "Chimera" text, he would have found the new evidence on page 3.

On that page Thomas Epach, former chief of the Criminal Division in the Cook County State's Attorney's office, addressed the sequence of events that put Simon in prison in place of Porter. Epach said, "It was Cook County's worst day. Nothing like this had ever happened before, certainly not in Cook County. Here an assistant Cook County prosecutor spends weeks before a grand jury calling witnesses and in the end proving once again that Porter, not Simon, committed the murders. Then a few weeks later that same prosecutor stands before the sentencing judge and doesn't utter a word about that evidence exculpating Simon as Simon is being sentenced to prison for Porter's crime."

Prior to the release of "Chimera," Epach's quote had never been cited publicly by any news organization anywhere. The chief of the Criminal Division when Simon was sent to Danville stated publicly that an innocent man had been sent to prison for thirty-seven years—and the *Tribune* editorial board wanted to know if Sotos and Ekl had any new evidence? When the quote was brought to the gathering's attention, Editor Dold smiled broadly, sat up in his chair, and said, "Tom Epach. I know Tom Epach."

No editorial of any kind came of that ninety-minute gathering.

I also gave copies of the most-sensitive materials underlying the Simon case to the editor of the *Chicago Sun-Times,* Jim Kirk, in the summer of 2013. Despite assurances that the paper would use the materials as the basis for a front-page piece about Simon and his possible innocence, the story never appeared.

I also attempted to contact key players in the state's attorney's office. I repeatedly requested an interview with Gainer, now an associate Cook County Criminal Court judge, about his own actions. I wanted to know why he told the sentencing judge, Fitzgerald, that he would call as key witnesses for the State three of the men at the Washington Park pool who had told the grand jury that Porter was the triggerman, but he did not. And I wanted to know why he said he would call Ciolino, who he knew had forced Simon's confession, but again he did not. My calls to Gainer were not just unsuccessful, they were met with threats of an immediate arrest.

In 2014, following such a request to Gainer, I received a call the following day from an individual identifying herself as a Chicago cop. She said she really did not want to drive to my suburban home with a warrant, and she asked me to cease making any more calls to Gainer. Two days following my last request of Gainer, at the end of January 2015, two Cook County Sheriff's police, assigned to the Criminal Intelligence Unit, came to my home and threatened to arrest me if the calls for an interview did not cease.

Regardless, by 2012 the ad hoc group began to coalesce around a resurgent effort to expose Medill's wrongdoing and to free Alstory Simon by proving his innocence. It should be admitted that while the group held to a common goal of freeing Simon, it was without any formal organization, and frequently its members lapsed into internecine bickering and strained relationships over strategies of how to best attain that ultimate goal. And, the squabbling was mixed in with a dose of plain old stumbling by members of the ad hoc group as well.

But momentum was building. Meaningfully, individuals who had been in the pool that night in 1982 and had witnessed Porter shoot his two victims began to come forward as word circulated that a genuine, renewed attempt to win freedom for Simon was at last gaining headway.

For example, Raymond D. Brown returned to Chicago in the summer of 2013 to appear in a short, televised news segment produced by Chuck Goudie, the ABC Channel Seven investigative reporter. Initially his was the sole Chicago media outlet to present the possibility of Simon's innocence. On camera, Brown told Goudie's audience that at the time of the shooting, he was twelve years old and was in the pool swimming with friends when he heard the sound of gunfire.

"I looked up to see Porter firing a gun and I saw Jerry lying in the bleachers," he said.

"I then saw Porter run past us with a gun in his hand. The gun appeared to be a large .38 caliber police gun. As Porter ran past us, we climbed over the fence and ran behind out of the pool area. I was a few feet behind Porter and could see the police gun in his hand."

The ad hoc group was provided with a huge lift in early 2011, though it proved to be ephemeral. Paul Pompian, a Chicago native who had moved to Southern California years before and had become a successful independent film producer, flew to Chicago after reading a copy of "Chimera," which had been sent to him by Marty Preib, the Chicago cop. Pompian declared himself a believer. Owner of Pompian Productions of Woodland Hills, California, Paul's credits included *Death of a Centerfold: The Dorothy Stratten Story* and *Swimming Upstream*. Paul had produced more than fifty other films and television productions, working first with New World Pictures and later with MGM.

Born and raised on Chicago's Southeast Side, Paul had worked a couple of years for Mayor Richard J. Daley in City Hall following graduation from Loyola University and thus was intimately familiar with the sometimes poisonous and duplicitous dynamics of Cook County politics. It was that experience that allowed him to understand how the Simon charade could have taken place.

Pompian began developing a prototype documentary about the Porter/Simon entanglement, an effort he was absolutely passionate about. During frequent trips to Chicago, Paul and a skilled videographer, along with other members of the ad hoc group traveled to Milwaukee to film an interview with the Reverend Robert Braun, the social activist with whom Simon had worked to shut down drug houses shortly after Simon, Inez, and the kids arrived in the Wisconsin city in 1982.

In the fall of 2011, five members of the team spent a night in a Danville motel before meeting Simon in a barren prison conference room the following morning. There a lengthy video interview was taken of a frequently tearful Simon trying to explain why he went along with the Ciolino-Protess-Rimland scheme.

The team also traveled to the south-suburban Summit home of Michael and Lisa Madonia to shoot an interview with the couple. (Michael Madonia recounted for the camera an incident in which Ciolino appeared at their front door and threatened to "put a hole" in Madonia's head if Madonia did not stop hassling one of Ciolino's clients. Rimland acted as Ciolino's attorney to defend the investigator against the ensuing misdemeanor charges, which were dropped in court in 2000.)

There were interviews filmed with Delorto, Mazzola, me, Ray Brown, on and on. Upon his return to his Woodland Hills, California, studios, Paul devoted himself 24/7 to stitching the video takes together in a coherent fashion. His goal was to present a polished, five-minute "trailer" to investors who would provide financing for a documentary.

He was driven to finish that documentary, but Paul died of leukemia in January 2014. The Alstory Simon documentary received a reprieve, however, when Shawn Rech, a producer and screen-writer from Cleveland, Ohio, who also had read "Chimera" and also believed in it, stepped in to continue Paul Pompian's project. He, too, interviewed Simon in Danville, the Reverend Braun in Milwaukee, and the others, but he went beyond Pompian's efforts by, among other things, hiring a small cadre of local actors to re-enact the pool shootings.

Word of Rech's efforts to take up where Pompian had left off circulated among an ever-widening media and political audience, including Cook County State's Attorney Anita Alvarez and her top aides. Simon's conviction was finally dismissed on October 30, 2014.

Cast
of Characters

ABRAMS, MARTIN: Chicago criminal defense attorney who was enlisted by Northwestern University's Medill School of Journalism professor David Protess to represent Inez Jackson. Jackson needed representation after she gave a 1999-videotaped confession that alleged her estranged husband, Alstory Simon, murdered two people in the pool area of Washington Park in 1982. Cook County prosecutors charged Inez with obstruction of justice.

ALVAREZ, ANITA: Cook County State's Attorney who agreed to review Alstory Simon's case and then announced on October 30, 2014, that Paul Biebel, presiding judge of the County's Criminal Division, had granted her request to immediately free Simon from prison. Her reason for the request was that the investigation of Simon's case had become so "corroded and corrupted" by a Northwestern journalism professor and others that justice demanded Simon's freedom.

ARMBRUST, SHAWN: former David Protess student at Northwestern University's Medill School of Journalism. Armbrust together with fellow students Thomas McCann, Syadene Rhodes-Pitts, and Cara Rubinsky believed they had uncovered new evidence in 1999 that proved that Anthony Porter was innocent of the 1982 Washington Park double homicide and that Alstory Simon was the real killer.

ARMSTRONG, KEN: *Chicago Tribune* reporter who with fellow *Tribune* reporter Maurice Possley published "Justice Derailed," a January 1999, five-part series that alleges prosecutors in Cook County State's Attorney Dick Devine's office—and prosecutors across the country—would either skirt the rules to win a conviction or were widely incompetent.

BECKWITH, EUGENE: witness with friends and fellow witnesses Kenneth Edwards, Mark Senior, and Michael Woodfork who were in the Washington Park pool area at the time of the 1982 shootings and who testified twice—at Anthony Porter's 1983 trial and before a 1999 grand jury—that they saw Porter shoot Marilyn Green and Jerry Hillard.

BODE, KEN: the former dean of Northwestern University's Medill School of Journalism who replaced Michael Janeway in the mid-1970s.

BRAUN, REVEREND ROBERT: Milwaukee social activist and friend of Alstory Simon who urged Simon not to plead guilty to a crime he did not commit. Simon's attorney, Jack Rimland, told Reverend Braun that Simon had to plead guilty because if he didn't, he was facing ninety-nine years in prison or even the death penalty.

CANNON, DIANE: criminal court judge who presided over a protracted hearing on whether notes and other materials Medill students had collected in the case of Anthony McKinney, a convicted killer, were protected by Illinois's shield law. Cannon ultimately ruled that the students were not reporters but in fact were working as investigators for McKinney's defense team who thus were required to surrender the materials to Cook County prosecutors.

CIOLINO, PAUL: licensed private detective who, working with David Protess, lectured Medill students on interviewing techniques. Ciolino extracted a videotaped statement from Alstory Simon in 1999 in which Simon confessed to the 1982 Washington Park double homicide.

CRAWFORD, WILLIAM B.: Pulitzer Prize-winning, former reporter for the *Chicago Tribune* who in 2009 and 2010 helped reenergize efforts to reopen Alstory Simon's case with the Internet publication of "Chimera," a 35,000-word account based on the records of the 1982 Washington Park double homicide. Crawford is also the author of this book.

DALEO, PAULA: assistant state's attorney in Cook County who with fellow assistant state's attorney Paul Szigetvari won the conviction of Anthony Porter following a short trial before Judge Robert Skoldowski in 1983.

DELO, STACY: former David Protess student at Northwestern University's Medill School of Journalism who with fellow students Stephanie Goldstein and Laura Sullivan in 1996 uncovered new evidence in the Ford Heights Four case that ultimately led to the four defendants' exoneration and release from prison.

DELORTO, JAMES: retired U.S. Alcohol, Tobacco and Firearms agent who with fellow retired ATF agent John Mazzola became a licensed private investigator. They were the first to suspect that Alstory Simon had been railroaded by Protess. They brought Simon's case files to the attention of two DuPage County attorneys who took on the Simon case pro bono.

DEVINE, RICHARD: Cook County State's Attorney when Alstory Simon confessed to the pool shootings in 1999. Under his watch Porter was quickly freed and Simon sentenced without a careful review of the evidence that originally convicted Porter or the circumstances of Simon's confession.

EDWARDS, KENNETH: witness with friends and fellow witnesses Eugene Beckworth, Mark Senior, and Michael Woodfork who were in the Washington Park pool area at the time of the 1982 shootings and who testified twice—at Anthony Porter's 1983 trial and before a 1999 grand jury—that they saw Anthony Porter shoot Marilyn Green and Jerry Hillard.

EKL, TERRY: DuPage County attorney who with fellow DuPage County attorney Jim Sotos agreed to represent the imprisoned Alstory Simon in his effort to win a hearing for his wrongful conviction after the case had been brought to their attention by former ATF agents James Delorto and John Mazzola.

EPACH, THOMAS: chief of the Criminal Division in the Cook County State's Attorney's office when Alstory Simon was sentenced in 1999, who signed a sworn affidavit in 2013 that alleged his boss, State's Attorney Dick Devine, allowed the sentencing to go forward despite questions that remained about the guilt of Simon and innocence of Porter.

FITZGERALD, THOMAS: Chief Judge of Cook County's Criminal Division who in 1999 sentenced Alstory Simon to thirty-seven years in prison after Simon entered a plea of guilty to the 1982 pool homicides.

FLAXMAN, KENNETH: Chicago attorney who in the mid-1980s threw the anti-death-penalty playbook at the state and federal judicial systems in a failed effort to win a new trial for Anthony Porter on the grounds that Flaxman had unearthed new evidence indicating Porter's innocence.

FORD HEIGHTS FOUR: Dennis Williams, William Rainge, Kenneth Adams, and Verneal Jimerson: four men who were convicted in 1978 of the rape and murder of twenty-three-year-old Carol Schmal and the murder of her fiancé, twenty-six-year-old Lawrence Lionberg, after the couple had been abducted from a Harvey, Illinois, gas station. The four men were exonerated and freed in 1996 as a result of the investigative efforts of Protess and three of his students.

GAINER, THOMAS: Cook County assistant state's attorney who represented the People of Illinois during the September 1999 sentencing of Alstory Simon and did not reveal to the sentencing judge key facts about the case.

GOLDSTEIN, STEPHANIE: former David Protess student at Northwestern University's Medill School of Journalism who in 1996 with fellow students Stacey Delo and Laura Sullivan uncovered new evidence in the Ford Heights Four case that ultimately led to the four defendants' exoneration and release from prison.

GRAY, DENNIS: Chicago police detective who with fellow Chicago police detective Charles Salvatore was assigned to Area One Violent Crimes and originally investigated the 1982 murders at the Washington Park pool. Their investigation led to the arrest of Anthony Porter on charges that he committed the double homicide.

GREEN, MARILYN: victim with her fiancé, Jerry Hilliard, when they were fatally shot on August 15, 1982, as they sat at the north end of the upper bleachers overlooking the Washington Park pool.

GREEN, OFFIE: Marilyn Green's mother who appeared at Alstory Simon's 1999 sentencing hearing, at the end of which Simon extended a lengthy apology to Offie for having fatally shot Marilyn.

GURSEL, AKIM: a criminal defense attorney who represented Anthony Porter at his 1983 criminal trial at the end of which Porter was found guilty and sentenced to die.

HALE, ANDY: coproducer with Shawn Rech of *Murder in the Park*, a documentary about how Simon was railroaded. The film was shown twice to Cook County prosecutors and helped Simon win a release from his wrongful incarceration in October 2014.

HILLIARD, JERRY: victim with his fiancée, Marilyn Green, when they were fatally shot on August 15, 1982, as they sat at the north end of the upper bleachers overlooking the Washington Park pool.

JACKSON, INEZ: estranged wife of Alstory Simon who in 1999 gave Ciolino, Protess, and a couple of Protess students a false statement, which was taped by Ciolino, in which she alleged that she witnessed Simon fatally shoot Marilyn Green and Jerry Hillard as the couple sat in the upper bleachers of the Washington Park pool area on August 15, 1982.

JACKSON, SONNY: son of Inez Jackson who agreed to help Protess identify Alstory Simon as the pool killer after Protess told Sonny, who was serving a lengthy prison sentence in Stanley, Wisconsin, that he would help Sonny get out of prison if Sonny helped Protess get Porter out of prison.

JACKSON, WALTER: nephew of Inez Simon who was visited in an Illinois prison by three Protess students and who agreed to sign an affidavit naming Alstory Simon as the pool killer after he had been promised by Protess that if he signed the affidavit, Protess would help him get out of jail.

JANEWAY, MICHAEL: the late dean of Northwestern University's Medill School of Journalism who was replaced by Ken Bode in the mid-1970s.

JONES, WALTER: criminal defense attorney who successfully represented the City of Chicago and two Chicago police detectives against a 2005 civil suit brought by Anthony Porter and his attorneys that asked a jury to award Porter $24 million in damages.

LAVINE, JOHN: former dean of the Medill School of Journalism at Northwestern University whose relatively brief tenure was marked by tension between himself and Protess. Lavine fired Protess in 2011 after an internal Medill investigation uncovered an array of wrongdoings by Protess.

LEWIS, EARL: state witness at Anthony Porter's sentencing hearing. Lewis testified that two weeks before the pool shootings in 1982, Porter kicked Lewis's dog without provocation, and after Lewis objected, Porter ducked into a neighboring building, returned with a handgun, and shot Lewis once in the head.

MAZZOLA, JOHN: retired U.S. Alcohol, Tobacco and Firearms agent who with fellow retired ATF agent James Delorto became licensed private investigators and were the first to suspect that Alstory Simon had been railroaded by Protess. They brought Simon's case files to the attention of two DuPage County attorneys who took on the Simon case pro bono.

McCANN, THOMAS: former David Protess student at Northwestern University's Medill School of Journalism. McCann together with fellow students Shawn Armbrust, Syadene Rhodes-Pitts, and Cara Rubinsky believed they had uncovered new evidence in 1999 that proved that Anthony Porter was innocent of the 1982 Washington Park double homicide and that Alstory Simon was the real killer.

McCRANEY, CHARLES: star government witness in the Ford Heights Four case who, years after the four men were convicted, was urged by David Protess and Paul Ciolino to change his testimony with the promise of a huge monetary award if he did.

McGHEE, DOUGLAS: state witness at Anthony Porter's sentencing hearing. McGhee testified that in 1979 he was in the bleachers of the Washington Park pool area when Porter beat him to a pulp in broad daylight, leaving him with a long-term injury and robbing him of $800.

McKINNEY, ANTHONY: convicted murderer for whom David Protess and his students were attempting to win a new trial for on the grounds they had uncovered new evidence suggesting his innocence in the slaying of a security guard years before. The effort backfired and in 2011 led to Protess's dismissal from Medill.

PORTER, ANTHONY: street gang member with a long history of violent crimes who was convicted in 1983 of the Washington Park double homicide. He was freed in 1999 by then-Cook County State's Attorney Dick Devine and subsequently pardoned by Illinois Governor George Ryan.

POSSLEY, MAURICE: *Chicago Tribune* reporter who with fellow *Tribune* reporter Ken Armstrong published "Justice Derailed," a January 1999, five-part series that alleges prosecutors in Cook County State's Attorney Dick Devine's office—and prosecutors across the country—would either skirt the rules to win a conviction or were widely incompetent.

PREIB, MARTY: Chicago police officer and published author whose tireless investigative efforts went a long way toward helping to win Simon's 2014 release from prison.

PROTESS, DAVID: long-time professor at Northwestern University's Medill School of Journalism who in 1999 founded the Innocence Project, which was dedicated to exposing cases where innocent individuals had been wrongfully convicted. The investigations were undertaken by Medill students. Protess was fired by Northwestern University in 2011 for withholding evidence and the truth from Medill colleagues, a Cook County judge, and his own attorney.

RECH, SHAWN: coproducer with Andy Hale of *Murder in the Park,* a documentary about how Simon was railroaded. The film was shown twice to Cook County prosecutors and helped Simon win a release from his wrongful incarceration in October 2014.

RHODES-PITTS, SYADENE: former David Protess student at Northwestern University's Medill School of Journalism. Rhodes-Pitts together with fellow students Shawn Armburst, Thomas McCann, and Cara Rubinsky believed they had uncovered new evidence in 1999 that proved that Anthony Porter was innocent of the 1982 Washington Park double homicide and that Alstory Simon was the real killer.

RIMLAND, JACK: criminal defense attorney who, at the request of Paul Ciolino, Rimland's officemate and friend, represented Alstory Simon for no fee during his September 1999 sentencing and misled his client and the judge about material facts of the case.

RUBINSKY, CARA: former David Protess student at Northwestern University's Medill School of Journalism. Rubinsky together with fellow students Shawn Armbrust, Thomas McCann, and Syadene Rhodes-Pitts believed they had uncovered new evidence in 1999 that proved that Anthony Porter was innocent of the 1982 Washington Park double homicide and that Alstory Simon was the real killer.

SALVATORE, CHARLES: Chicago police detective who with fellow Chicago police detective Dennis Gray was assigned to Area One Violent Crimes and originally investigated the 1982 pool murders. Their investigation led to the arrest of Anthony Porter on charges that he committed the double homicide.

SENIOR, MARK: witness with friends and fellow witnesses Eugene Beckworth, Kenneth Edwards, and Michael Woodfork who were in the Washington Park pool area at the time of the 1982 shootings and who testified twice—at Anthony Porter's 1983 trial and before a 1999 grand jury—that they saw Anthony Porter shoot Marilyn Green and Jerry Hillard.

SIMON, ALSTORY: the centerpiece of the story who, as a consequence of a sinisterly brilliant scheme inspired by Protess and brought to fruition by Protess, private eye Paul Ciolino and Simon's attorney Jack Rimland, was tricked into pleading guilty to the 1982 pool murders through promises he would do only two years in prison and receive huge monetary awards upon his release. Simon served more than fifteen years and left prison penniless.

SKOLDOWSKI, ROBERT: presiding criminal court judge at Anthony Porter's 1983 trial who sentenced Porter to death after a jury found him guilty of the pool homicides. After a post-trial hearing, Skoldowski found Porter to be a fit candidate for the death penalty.

SOTOS, JIM: DuPage County attorney who with fellow DuPage County attorney Terry Ekl agreed to represent the imprisoned Alstory Simon in his effort to win a hearing for his wrongful conviction after the case had been brought to their attention by former ATF agents James Delorto and John Mazzola.

STACK, CELESTE: long-serving Cook County assistant state's attorney who headed the office's Conviction Integrity Unit. Stack was one of two witnesses called before a March 1999 Cook County grand jury that indicted Alstory Simon on double homicide charges.

SULLIVAN, LAURA: former David Protess student at Northwestern University's Medill School of Journalism who in 1996 with Stacy Delo and Stephanie Goldstein uncovered new evidence in the Ford Heights Four case that ultimately led to the four defendants' exoneration and release from prison.

SZIGETVARI, PAUL: assistant state's attorney in Cook County who with fellow assistant state's attorney Paula Daleo won the conviction of Anthony Porter following a short trial before Judge Robert Skoldowski in 1983.

SZUDARSKI, ALLEN: retired Chicago Police Department detective who was one of only two witnesses called before a March 1999 Cook County grand jury that indicted Alstory Simon on double homicide charges.

TAYLOR, WILLIAM: key state witness who helped convict Anthony Porter at Porter's 1983 jury trial but who, in 1998, supplied Medill student Thomas McCann and investigator Paul Ciolino with a sworn affidavit suggesting that he had not actually seen Porter shoot the Washington Park pool victims.

WARDEN, ROB: head of Northwestern University Law School's Center on Wrongful Convictions, which he cofounded, and a former Chicago journalist who once owned *Chicago Lawyer,* a monthly tabloid that closely tracked Chicago's legal community.

WOODFORK, MICHAEL: witness with friends and fellow witnesses Eugene Beckwith, Kenneth Edwards, and Mark Senior who were in the Washington Park pool at the time of the 1982 shootings and who testified twice—at Anthony Porter's 1983 trial and before a 1999 grand jury—that they saw Anthony Porter shoot Marilyn Green and Jerry Hillard.

ZORN, ERIC: *Chicago Tribune* columnist and a supporter of David Protess, his students, and the Innocence Project and their dogged efforts to win the release of wrongfully convicted defendants who had been convicted of violent crimes and sentenced to long prison terms.

About
the Author

Photograph by William Crawford III

William B. Crawford is a former reporter, writer and legal affairs columnist for the *Chicago Tribune*. During a twenty-three-year career at the newspaper, he was the recipient of a Pulitzer Prize as well as many other major awards for his work. After leaving the newspaper, he was the Chicago Mercantile Exchange's senior vice president of global communications. In 2002, he co-founded O'Connell & Crawford LLC, a media strategy and crisis management firm. *Justice Perverted: How The Innocence Project at Northwestern University's Medill School of Journalism Sent an Innocent Man to Prison* is Crawford's second book. His first was a thriller novel, *Rent Asunder*.

Printed in Poland
by Amazon Fulfillment
Poland Sp. z o.o., Wrocław